"This book is an excellent example of the fine tradition of muckraking, a style which has made a serious contribution to analysis, consciousness and social change uniquely in North America. But implicit in the manuscript is a more profound message, i.e. that though David may kill the Goliath Cargill, still all will not be well since there is a deeper social structure (which Cargill exemplifies) that needs changing."

> – *Robert Stirling, Dept. of Sociology, University of Regina*

"The alternative to the Wheat Board and the Pools is often painted as a system of smaller, more aggressive, 'entrepreneurial' organizations. It is not. The alternative is Cargill and similar multinationals which are far larger than the Board or any Canadian grain company. It is an open question which alternative is more consistent with the self-reliant, free-enterprise philosophy held by most Prairie farmers. Brewster Kneen's review of Cargill's growth and activities will help in finding an answer."

> – *John Morriss, Publisher and Editor, <u>The Manitoba Co-operator</u>*

"Brewster Kneen has finally done it. He has pulled together a comprehensive analysis of the international grain cartel's leading member, Cargill Inc., in one place. Although Cargill normally shrouds its activities in secrecy, Kneen has exposed them to the light of day. What can be seen is very, very disturbing. As one farmer put it recently, 'Companies like Cargill could give capitalism a bad name'."

> – *Mark Ritchie, Policy Advisor, Minnesota Dept. of Agriculture*

TRADING UP

How Cargill, the World's Largest
Grain Trading Company, Is Changing
Canadian Agriculture

Brewster Kneen

NC PRESS LTD.

Toronto, 1990

Front cover: Lintlaw, Saskatchewan
All photographs by Brewster Kneen
Editing, artwork, and design: Cathleen Kneen

Canadian Cataloguing in Publication Data

Main entry under title:

Trading up: how Cargill, the world's largest grain company, is changing
Canadian agriculture

Includes bibliographical references.
ISBN 1-55021-060-2

1. Cargill Incorporated.   2. Grain trade – Canada.
I. Title.

HD9044.C24C35   1990   338.7'6331'0971   C90-093948-6

We would like to thank the Ontario Arts Council and the Canada
Council for their assistance in the production of this book.

New Canada Publications, a division of NC Press Limited,
Box 452, Station A, Toronto, Ontario, Canada, M5W 1H8.

Distributed in the United States of America by Seven Hills
Books Distributors, 49 Central Ave., Cincinnati, Ohio 45202.

Printed and bound in Canada

This book is dedicated to all the farmers who believe a sustainable food system can and should be built on the principles of equity and justice.

My thanks to all those whose files, notes, and conversations contributed to the research for this study, including Cargill employees. I have tried to give credit where it is due, but unfortunately many of those whose work and whose insights appear in these pages must remain anonymous. I am particularly grateful to those whose critical reading of various drafts of this work added much to its accuracy and clarity and to the identification of the issues at stake. I am very aware that research of this sort is a collective endeavour. If there are errors, they are mine.

Finally, a word of very special thanks to my most demanding editor and critic, Cathleen, for her diligence and dedication to seeing this project through.

CONTENTS

SECTION I: INTRODUCTION

A Story of Cargill, Inc.   1
Picking on Cargill   3
Chapter 1: Open For Business   7

SECTION II: THE CONTEXT

Chapter 2: The Canadian Grain Marketing System   13
    The Canadian Wheat Board
    The Prairie Pools
    Grain Handling
    Grain Marketing
    National Grains Bureau
    Palliser/Western Canadian Wheat Growers Association
    Wheat Marketing in Ontario

Chapter 3: Peer Pressure   27

SECTION III: CARGILL'S DEVELOPMENT

Chapter 4: Long Term, Long View   31
    Private Ownership and Control
    Cargill's Structure
    International Structure and Finances
    Information Systems

Chapter 5: Riding the Gravy Train   41

Chapter 6: Deep Pockets   47

SECTION IV: CARGILL IN CANADA

Chapter 7: Historic Development   51
    (Chronology)

Chapter 8: Nuts and Bolts   57
    Fertilizer
    Mills and Elevators
    Meat

Chapter 9: Ontario: A Place to Grow   69
     Beans and Corn
     Terms of Trade
     The Seed Business

Chapter 10: Personnel and Politics   79

SECTION V: MOVIN' IT

Chapter 11: Transportation   89
     The Canadian Grain Transportation System

SECTION VI: SHAKIN' IT

Chapter 12: Transportation Policy   93
     Railways: Capturing Subsidies

Chapter 13: Grains Policy   103
     A Bigger Slice of the Export Pie
     Making Sure There Is Too Much

Chapter 14: Public Policy   111

SECTION VII: MAKING CHOICES

Chapter 15: Conclusion   117

Endnotes   127
Bibliography   131
Index   134

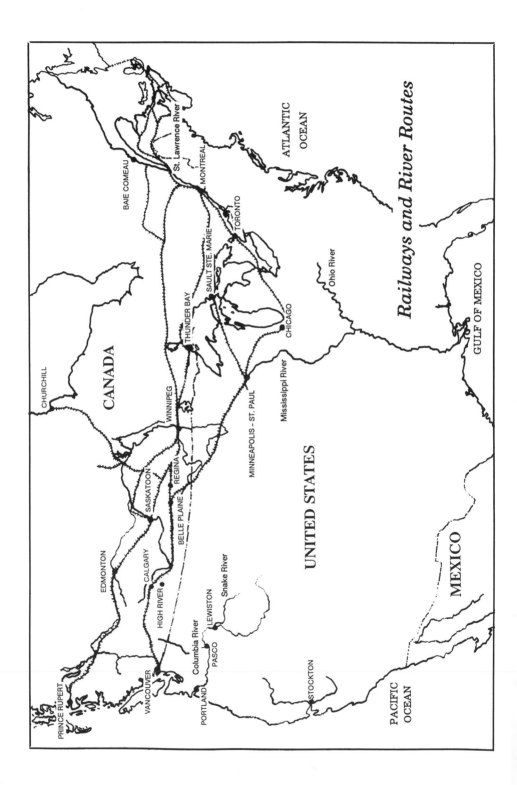

Railways and River Routes

ATLANTIC OCEAN

GULF OF MEXICO

St. Lawrence River

BAIE COMEAU

MONTREAL

TORONTO

SAULT STE. MARIE

THUNDER BAY

CHICAGO

Ohio River

CHURCHILL

CANADA

WINNIPEG

Mississippi River

MINNEAPOLIS - ST. PAUL

SASKATOON

REGINA

BELLE PLAINE

UNITED STATES

EDMONTON

CALGARY

HIGH RIVER

Snake River

LEWISTON

Columbia River

PASCO

STOCKTON

MEXICO

PRINCE RUPERT

VANCOUVER

PORTLAND

PACIFIC OCEAN

A STORY OF CARGILL, INC.

... the world's largest grain trader

and the world's "largest family-owned business"

Cargill:	world's largest grain trader
	world's tenth largest seed company
in the U.S.A.	
Cargill is the	largest private corporation
	largest egg producer (until mid-1989)
	largest soybean crusher
	largest feedlot operator
	second or third largest meat packer
	third largest flour miller

> Cargill and its subsidiaries and affiliates operate from approximately 800 locations in 55 countries with approximately 46,000 employees worldwide. Approximately 40% of Cargill's net worth is invested outside the United States: a similar percentage of its sales volume is generated by international operations. [1]

Cargill's global operations are directed from its headquarters in the Minneapolis, Minnesota, suburb of Minnetonka.

In 1989, *Forbes* magazine listed Cargill, Inc., as the largest private company in America with revenues in 1988 and 1989 of $43-billion each year. It employs 53,710 people.[2]

Sales of Cargill Inc.		
	1971 –	$2-billion
	1981 –	29-billion
	1986 –	32-billion
	1989 –	43-billion

NOTE: It must be assumed that these figures are the global sales of Cargill Inc. and its subsidiaries. Even the figures given by Forbes *are not consistent in either numbers or the way they are identified. This may be attributed to the fact that for a private corporation operating globally, there is no way to get accurate and consistent figures from one source, and no country requires such reporting by private corporations.*

And in Canada?

"Our experience is if you're too big, people don't want to do business with you." – Kerry Hawkins, president, Cargill Ltd. [3]

- Cargill operates grain handling facilities at 105 locations in western Canada;
- Cargill operates 23 primary elevators in Ontario and 2 in Quebec;
- Cargill handles 14% of Ontario's grain production and 8% of the western Canadian crop. [4]

Cargill's Canadian operations are directed from the Winnipeg, Manitoba, offices of its wholly-owned subsidiary, Cargill Ltd. Its Canadian sales total about $1.5-billion annually and at the end of 1989 Cargill employed 1500 people in Canada. At that time it had offices and facilities from Vancouver, British Columbia, to Moncton, New Brunswick.

It could be said that Cargill is a small player in Canada. The three Prairie Pools (Alberta, Saskatchewan, and Manitoba) handle 80% of Canada's grain at the collection stage while Cargill handles 8-9%. However, with the Canadian government pushing as hard and as fast as it can to de-regulate, privatize and do away with any and all structures that allow some social control to be exercised over The Market, there is little reason to rest secure in the strength of the Pools or the Canadian Wheat Board.

Introduction

PICKING ON CARGILL

The men had their arms folded across their chests so we could not see the Cargill logo on their shirts. They were complaining about an educational display we had erected at a large Ontario rural exhibition. All it contained were some pictures of Cargill facilities, from the Thunder Bay terminal to some of the newly-acquired feed mills in various parts of Ontario, along with some data on the extent of Cargill's operations around the world. But they were certainly upset! "Why are you picking on Cargill?" they demanded.

Such hostility and defensiveness provoked by the public display of simple facts about a major corporate presence in Canada invites deeper probing into the affairs, policies and practices of that corporation. This is not mere curiosity. Understanding its mission and its intents as well as its day to day customs and attitudes is a public responsibility. I also hope this will form a base on which everyone affected by developments in the food system will be able to make more informed and more socially responsible decisions about our common future.

Cargill is important to grain, and grain is important to Canada: Canada produces 4 percent of the world's total wheat production and Canada's wheat exports make up 20 percent of the world's wheat trade. Since the early 1970s, five countries/regions – the United States, the European Community, Argentina, Australia, and Canada – have accounted for over 75 percent of the world's wheat exports. Cargill by itself is said to control some 25 percent of the total world trade.

These statistics, however, do not reveal what is really at stake in the growing struggle over control of Canadian agriculture in general and prairie grain production in particular.

The drive to settle the West came more from the need for cheap food for the industrial workforce of Britain and, later, Upper Canada, than from a vision of a just and sustainable economy. The wheat economy of the Prairies was, in effect, created by the capital and power concentrated in the industrializing centres. The consequences of this concentrated economic and political power in the early years of this century convinced the Prairie settlers that they had to gain control over the marketing of what they produced. It was not enough to own their own land and have control over the means of production if this control was nullified once the crop left the farm gate.

The experience of pillage and exploitation at the hands of the railroads, the merchants and the bankers drove the prairie farmers to fight for and establish the provincial wheat pools, the Canadian Wheat Board, an equitable financing system and an equitable transportation policy to govern the railroads, as well as the provincial governments that would support and legislate these matters. The federal government had to accomodate itself to their power.

In recent years the tide has been turning against the people of the Prairies and the institutions they struggled to build. The struggle is not confined to the Prairies, however, because the contenders for power and control transcend provincial and national boundaries and their ambition appears to know no limits. What they advertise, of course, is not their ambition – or what some might call their greed – but their "competitiveness" and their "efficiency". These contenders for power are the transnational corporations that constitute oligopolies in every sector of the food system, the commodity groups that are established to do their bidding and market their ideology,   their academic apologists, and their government agents, represented currently by the Conservative federal government in Ottawa as well as by the Tory governments in the provinces of Alberta, Saskatchewan and Manitoba.

The loud segment of the farming population who have always believed in the macho individualist cowboy image and the mythology of the capitalist entrepreneur should not be allowed to obscure the social and economic history that created institutions like the Pools and the Canadian Wheat Board, and created human communities in the face of Prairie isolation and adversity.

> Given the typical boom and bust cycle of the world demand and supply of farm products, it is impossible to predict the future with any degree of certainty.[5]

> The future of the grain economy of the Prairies is as much dependent on government policy as on anything else. . . The most influential governments in the export markets are the United States and the European Community. Canadian grain farmers face an uncertain future because of lack of knowledge or control of these major forces in the grain markets of the world. [6]

Such statements are typical of virtually all public discussion of agriculture in general and grain in particular. Among the "major forces in the grain markets of the world" the private transnational corporations are neither named nor analyzed. The quotes above are from two of several financed, in part, by Cargill for the government-funded Economic Council of Canada. This may be why the corporate sector in general, and Cargill in particular, remain un-named and absent from the analysis. It may also be because Cargill was also represented on the advisory committee of the Economic Council which directed these studies.

The Council, in its own report in 1988, commented that:

> There have been major changes in the configuration of the grain and oilseed trade over the [past] two and a half decades with regard to both actors and commodities.[7]

Yet in none of its studies or reports is the major actor identified, much less its role analyzed. Cargill, Ltd. is now emerging as the most significant single actor in the formation of agricultural policy in Canada – and possibly in the world. There are other actors, of course, but none appear to wield the same influence or to be so sure of what they want to achieve.

Chapter 1

OPEN FOR BUSINESS

When I started this study many months ago, I was surprised to discover that while Cargill, and other corporations of its size and significance, had been closely watched during the 1960s and '70s, the files appear to have been closed since about 1979, when critical research turned primarily to the activities and policies of national governments. One might interpret this as a reflection of the metamorphosis of the corporation into the state – the larva turning into a butterfly. In other words, the state has become the effective agent of the corporation. Of course this is an over-simplification, but the complexities and contradictions in the administration of any government should not be permitted to obscure the effective structure of power: in Canada, a cosy mixture of elected parliamentarians of the ruling party and high-level bureaucrats and administrators. If there is in fact a conflation of corporate with state interests and power, then it is imperative to focus once again on the corporate sector as more than simple lobbyists for government favour.

Disclaimers to the contrary, it appears that the role of the corporate sector in general, and Cargill in particular, in the affairs of the Canadian government has been intimate for many years. As I probed into the past twenty years of agricultural policy, and of the transformation of agriculture into agri-business, I discovered that Cargill and its corporate and ideological companions seem to have been the major architects of Canadian agricultural and transportation policy and practice. Certainly since the Tory sweep of 1984 there has been a dramatic increase in the determination of public policy by the corporate sector, its ideological high priests in organizations like the Business Council on National Issues, and its indentured servants in government and the universities.

This fundamental shift in government orientation was marked by the Prime Minister's statement, shortly after assuming office in 1984, that *"Canada is open for business."* The Foreign Investment Review Agency – the tool the Liberals had created to keep a hand on foreign control of the Canadian economy – was turned upside down and renamed Investment Canada, the equivalent to a declaration of prostitution. Cargill, as we will see, wasted little time in responding to the invitation.

Imagine the Wheat Board, and the farmer-owned and controlled Prairie co-operatives (the Pools) that handle 80% of Canadian grain, as a table around which all the participants in the grain business gather to enjoy reasonably equitable participation in the meal. Now imagine the family dog, no longer willing to accept only the crumbs which fall from the table, chewing conscientiously at first one leg and then another of the table. In 1990, government assurances to the contrary, it appears that the table could well collapse because of the damage done by the incessant nibbling away at its supports. Cargill is waiting for more than just the scraps to fall into its dish.

This scenario shows only one aspect of a complex picture, of course. Cargill always plays it safe, whether in trading (by hedging its buying and selling) or in policy formation. While it may be seeking the eventual destruction of the Canadian Wheat Board, at the same time it is working with it to obtain as much of the grain trade as it can under the circumstances. (Even the far-right groups do not *directly* attack the Wheat Board.)

Method

To get to know a company like Cargill it is not enough to go to the libraries and to write away for corporate reports. The corporate reports do not exist because the company is private, and the libraries contain only fragments of information. The example of the Toronto Metropolitan Library illustrates the challenge: through no fault of a very helpful staff, there is virtually no information in the business section on Cargill, and a $50 computer search of newspapers and periodicals failed to turn up anything I had not already found through my own newspaper clipping and periodical survey. Even the Canadian Wheat Board library had only one book I had not found anywhere else and no files on Cargill.

In order to interpret what little hard data is available, and to get a picture of how such a company actually works, it is necessary to talk with employees, competitors, government regulators and neighbours. In addition to gathering this oral history, it is also important to analyze maps and facilities, to view the world from the perspective of corporate headquarters. This perspective may also be gained directly through conversations with corporate executives and their employees.

In trying to gather information for this study I have talked with many individuals in all aspects of the grain trade, and tried to talk with many more. I found Cargill people very often quite accessible and easy to talk with, particularly local managers. The problem with this approach, however, is that few Cargill employees know very much about the company they work for. Frequently local managers have said, "I would like to see the book when it is finished. I would like to know more about Cargill myself."

Talking with competitors is also helpful, and equally frustrating: "Cargill? I have to do business with them." Thus begins and ends yet another interview with someone in the grain business, in this case an executive of the Ontario Wheat Marketing Board.

This book, therefore, represents only a piece of the "Cargill study" that remains to be done. I have looked in detail only at

Cargill's development and role in Canada. To complete the picture, others will have to assemble their own pieces of the jig-saw puzzle and fit them together. Even while I was writing this, for example, a farmer who heard I was working on Cargill called to tell me that when he received a Christmas greeting from what he thought was his locally-owned fertilizer and feed supplier he was casually notified that the firm was now owned by Cargill. In another small town, Cargill's Season's Greeting is that the local elevator will be torn down.

What difference does it make if Cargill owns the local mill, instead of the Brown family, or the local fertilizer plant, instead of a couple of local brothers? By whom and for what reasons was the decision made to tear down the elevator? Such questions must be answered by those who live in those situations.

Gaining an understanding of how the system works is not nearly as mysterious as it is made out to be by those who profit from public confusion, even though it is a virtually endless process. I know that this book will not be up-to-date when it is published because Cargill will not stand still long enough. The important point is the accuracy of the structural analysis. There are all sorts of salacious stories about Cargill – of the sort one can probably uncover in any other major corporation, about fraud, labour relations, and so on – but you will not find them in this book. What you will find is a framework, and a method, which can be used to illuminate not only Cargill in Canada, but the whole system of corporate capitalism wherever in the world it operates.

The Role of Ideology

The big don't get that way by waiting around for something to happen. – F.J. Ackerman, Louis Dreyfus Canada Ltd.

One place to begin is reading between the lines of what is published, as illustrated in the studies done for the Economic Council of Canada cited above *(page 5)*. What else is being said, in addition to the words on the page? Note also the use of the future tense. This is a technique of mystification. Events don't just "happen", anonymously and mysteriously, as is implied when people say that this or that will happen without any suggestion that there might be some agency involved, some subject that has a hand in making the events happen.

Anonymity, however, can serve many purposes. It is a good way to avoid responsibility and, with it, questions of power and control.

The problem, in its essence, is our acceptance of the *invisible hand*, a concept created by Adam Smith nearly two hundred years ago, that supposedly guides history and makes everything turn out for the best if only we allow it to function without restraint. This is the theory behind the ideology of the Market Economy: that every individual seeking to satisfy their individual interests will produce the best possible society. Another term that describes this ideology is *social Darwinism*, the doctrine of the survival of the fittest. Social Darwinism combined with the invisible hand provide the ideological rationale for the political program of extreme individualism and the so-called *free market* behind which the corporate sector operates. In this doctrine, anything that interferes with the rampant expression of individualism is immoral. Hence the moral imperatives of *efficiency* and *competition* that infest government and corporate language today. (I have explained social Darwinism more fully in my book *From Land to Mouth*.)

What we are schooled to overlook is that the invisible hand is attached to an arm, and that arm to a body which is controlled by an active mind. We are also schooled to overlook the fact that the determinist philosophy of the invisible hand absolutely contradicts the mythology of free enterprise and initiative. You cannot have it both ways.

Cargill, global grain trader – Cargill, global commodity merchant – Cargill, fertilizer maker, meat packer – Cargill, advisor to governments – and Cargill, beneficiary of massive public subsidies – is as good a corporation as any to illustrate the characteristics of anonymity, individualism, and determinism. If there is any corporation that tries to have it both ways, that champions the free market *and* accepts every possible government handout and public benefit – it is Cargill.

This is not to demonize Cargill or to resort to a conspiracy theory of history. As I said, there are any number of other corporations one could analyze, and Cargill is not really conspiring – at least I do not think it is – but is simply playing the current game with exceptional skill. Nevertheless, one does have to begin somewhere to shatter the myth of anonymity and determinism. Cargill can be known, and might even be held accountable for what it does and for the policies of which it has been and continues to be the agent. This might be a far sounder background against which to discuss public policy than an environment in which the pretence prevails that the government creates policy and the corporate sector does not exist.

If the resulting study presents "a case", as one agricultural scientist suggested, then it is probably wise to consider the merits of the case. To refuse consideration of the whole case as presented by the data available together with their interpretation is to slip back into the social Darwinism of irresponsibility that claims that events just *happen*. The reader must judge whether the "case" I present here stands up or not. Many times in the course of working on this I have had to go back to information I thought was irrelevant and reconsider it in the light of what I had subsequently learned. Considered in a reductionist mode, as discrete bits of information, events cannot be identified as cause and effect. It is only in the context of looking at historic developments, at relationships and changes, that cause and effect become discernable or even discussable. It is on the far side of such critical analysis that action, with power, becomes possible.

A note about statistics: I have tried to ensure that the figures presented here are as accurate as possible. I have, however, come up against irreconcilable discrepancies when I have been forced, due to scarcity of information, to present composite figures drawn from a variety of sources. I have tried to err on the conservative side in every case of such discrepancies. In addition, while it may appear that there are discrepancies between figures given for apparently the same items, a careful reading may indicate, for example, that one figure is for Prairie grain, while another includes Prairie and Ontario grain; and in some cases figures are for all grains while in others they are for wheat only, or only for export grains.

SECTION II: THE CONTEXT

Chapter 2

THE CANADIAN GRAIN MARKETING SYSTEM

~~~~~~

The Canadian Wheat Board

All wheat grown in Manitoba, Saskatchewan, Alberta and the Peace River area of British Columbia, and destined either for the export market or for human consumption within Canada, is marketed solely by the Canadian Wheat Board. At different times in the past, oats and barley have also come under the jurisdiction of the Wheat Board.

Established in 1935, the Canadian Wheat Board is "a unique blend of public and private enterprise. While its powers are granted by government, its formation and continued operation is the result of support by grain producers themselves, who finance all costs of the Board's operations."[8]

The Canadian Wheat Board is directed by government-appointed commissioners, who are advised by a committee of elected producers. Initially a voluntary marketing agency for prairie wheat, it acquired compulsory marketing powers for wheat in 1943, under the War Measures Act, as a means of enforcing wartime price controls. In 1949 the Board's powers were extended, by a change in the regulations of its governing Act, to oats and barley, and at that time it covered all of those three grains from the designated area, including that which was sold for livestock feed.

The Wheat Board uses a system of initial and final grain payments to ensure equity among grain farmers, regardless of where they live and when and where they deliver their grain. The initial price serves as a price guarantee, with the final payment made only after grain is actually sold and all costs covered. The result is a common, or *pooled*, price for all grain of like grade in any crop year.

Delivery quotas are also a part of this marketing system, ensuring that each farmer has fair access to the elevator system. The amount producers can deliver on a particular quota is based on each producer's indication to the Board of how many acres in the coming crop year are being assigned to the different grains. Each farm is issued, annually, a Wheat Board delivery permit book based on these figures. There are no restrictions or incentives for the production of any type of grain in Western Canada, but the use of delivery quotas does allow the Board to match available supplies with sales by regulating the timing of grain deliveries.

The Wheat Board does not own or operate physical marketing facilities but uses, as agents, the various private and co-operative grain handling companies. Grain for export may also be sold through accredited exporters (including the major Canadian grain handling companies and international grain trading companies). However, the Wheat Board's direct sales, generally to state trading companies, account for 80-85% of Canadian grain exports.

Unlike the private grain trading corporations, the CWB does not have a significant capital base. Rather than having the goal of maximizing profit for the corporation, the Wheat Board exists to maximize the return to the primary producer on an equitable basis.

The Prairie Pools

Unique to Canada, and arising out of a combination of social-ist and populist traditions and the desperate situation prairie farmers found themselves in during the 1920s, are the prairie pools: The Alberta Wheat Pool, founded in 1923, the Saskatchewan Wheat Pool, founded in 1923, and Manitoba Pool Elevators, founded in 1924. The pools were strong supporters of the establishment of the Canadian Wheat Board.

Today the pools are farmer-owned cooperatives which col-lectively handle 80-85% of western wheat production. They own and operate both country and terminal grain elevators and are involved in a variety of businesses, both singly and together. They have an extensive democratic structure and endeavour to reflect the wishes and interests of their members, though one can frequently hear the criticism that they have "gotten too big" and act just like other corporations. However, because of their purpose, which is not to accumulate capital but to serve their members, they have only a minimal capital base and nothing like the power, and the freedom to manoeuver and manipulate, that private corporations may have.

Grain Handling

Once grain has been harvested, it is stored on-farm or deliv-ered to a local, or *primary*, elevator (like the one by an abandoned siding on the cover of this book). Country elevators have been a central element of both the Prairie landscape and the grain han-dling system for at least seventy years.

Primary elevators accept grain from producers either on be-half of the Canadian Wheat Board or the company which owns the elevator. They weigh, sample, grade and *elevate* – place into their elevator, or silo – the grain. Subsequently this grain is loaded into railway cars and and sent either east or west to a ter-minal elevator from which it is exported.

The various elevators and grain dealers for western grain are licensed by the Canadian Grain Commission, which also has regulatory authority over the quality of Canadian grain and over its handling, transportation and storage system. The Canadian Grain Commission, established in 1912, is responsible to the Minister of State for the Canadian Wheat Board – Charlie Mayer under the Conservatives – who reports to Parliament. The Commissioners are appointed by Governor-in-Council (Cabinet).

The Canadian Grain Commission should not be confused with the Canada Grains Council, which represents the interests of the corporate sector in the grain industry. Its membership ranges from Cargill and Continental Grain to the the Winnipeg Grain Exchange and the Western Canadian Wheat Growers Association. It does not include the three prairie Pools, but it does include United Grain Growers, a right-wing farmers' co-operative. It also includes as associate members Cyanamid Canada and the Royal Bank.

As of August, 1989, according to the Commission, ownership of primary elevators in the prairie region was as follows:

	number	storage capacity, tonnes
Saskatchewan Wheat Pool	490	1,877,970
Alberta Wheat Pool	276	1,503,270
United Grain Growers	291	1,178,690
Pioneer Grain		
(James Richardson & Sons)	205	883,390
Manitoba Pool Elevators	143	555,870
Cargill Ltd.	106	467,710
Parrish & Heimbecker	32	235,910
N.M.Paterson & Sons	52	211,440
other	24	209,480

Against a total of 1619 primary elevators, there are only 22 terminal elevators, most of them located in Vancouver and Prince Rupert, British Columbia, and Thunder Bay, Ontario, and owned by the pools, either singly or as a consortium, or by private traders like Cargill. (The initial owners of the Prince Rupert grain terminal (1982) included the three pools, UGG, Cargill and Pioneer. The Alberta and Saskatchewan pools held 34 and 30% respectively.)[9]

Of the 22 terminal elevators, four are "inland terminals" that were built and operated by the federal government but privatized by the Liberal government in which Otto Lang was the Minister Responsible for Grains and Oilseeds. Terminal elevators are much larger than the primary elevators; essentially they accept grain from the primary elevators and accumulate it for export.

Grain Marketing

In 1970 the three Pools and United Grain Growers combined to form XCAN Grain Ltd. to market grain abroad. This was done only when it had become clear that the powers of the Wheat Board would not be expanded and that the federal government would require the Board to continue to depend on private agents for much of its sales. Because of competition between UGG and the Pools, the three Pools bought UGG's share of XCAN in 1973-4 by mutual agreement.[10]

In 1973 the Canadian Government established a two-price system for milling wheat in Canada. In its first years of operation, the fixed price for milling wheat was subsidized by the federal government so that while farmers were being paid $5.00 per bushel through the Wheat Board, the millers were paying a subsidized price of only $3.25. When export grain prices dropped, and stayed low, the subsidy went to the farmers instead of the millers. For example, in 1975, when the export price was $2.25, the millers were paying $3.55 for wheat while the farmers were being paid $5 per bushel for milling wheat by the Wheat Board. The Federal Government made up the difference. Due to continuing low grain prices, it stayed that way until the two-price system was ended by the Federal Government in 1988 as part of its trade deal with the U.S.A., and after a one-year transition period, farmers received the same price for export as for domestic milling wheat.

In 1974 the federal government ended the Wheat Board's monopoly over grades of wheat, oats and barley that were sold for livestock feed within Canada, allowing them to be traded on the open market. In January, 1989, it was announced by the Minister

Responsible for Grains and Oilseeds, Charlie Mayer, (also responsible for the Wheat Board) that oats would be removed from Wheat Board jurisdiction altogether on August 1st.

Contrary to popular understanding of Canada's parliamentary democracy, decisions concerning agricultural policy are not made by Parliament, or with public debate, but rather by the Federal Cabinet after consultation with those it chooses to listen to. (see p. 25) In announcing the Cabinet decision, Mayer explained that the best way to market oats "is with individuals and private traders." Among the supporters of this decision were the Western Canadian Wheat Growers Association and Cargill Ltd., who praised the Wheat Board for its "leadership" in the decision. The Wheat Board, however, immediately issued a statement contradicting Cargill and pointing out that the federal cabinet made the decision, which was not based on any request from the Wheat Board.[11]

As indicated earlier, the removal of first barley and then oats from Wheat Board jurisdiction was possible, without legislative change, because both had been included under Wheat Board jurisdiction in the first place under the *regulations* of the Act, not the Act itself. This makes it obvious that nothing that is not in the Act itself is secure in the face of continuing pressure to undermine the authority and scope of the Wheat Board.

It must be pointed out, in the case of oats, that the action of the Minister responsible was undertaken without even consulting with the Wheat Board advisory committee. It was also against the policy of the Saskatchewan Wheat Pool, which reconfirmed its position at the annual delegates meeting in November, 1989, that "All grains and oilseeds should be marketed by the Canadian Wheat Board, providing this is demonstrated to be the wishes of the majority of the producers, and with the exception of farm to farm, farm to feedlot, and farm to feedmill sales."

At that same meeting, Pool delegates also reaffirmed their support of "the concept of single desk selling as a critical aspect of the CWB's operations" and called for the federal government to "amend the Canadian Wheat Board Act to formally put barley under Board control and return oats to its control."[12]

Another aspect of Canada's grain marketing system which has been swept aside by the Tory administration without legislative involvement was the interest-free cash advance to farmers. This was an advance available to CWB shippers on the basis of their grain production at the time of harvest up to a limit of $30,000, so that no one would be penalized for holding their grain until it was called for by the marketing system. The grain stored on-farm constituted the collateral for the loan, and the value of the loan was deducted from the initial payment for the grain made at the time the grain was delivered to the country elevator.

In the fall of 1989 the government, without consultation with the farmers involved, announced that henceforth interest would be charged on the cash advance, thus defeating the intent of the program, which was to achieve equity and equality among grain farmers on the prairies. Removal of the interest-free cash advance will mean that everyone will try to deliver their grain as early as possible, and those who have to wait will be penalized. This is, probably not by accident, a good way to foment dissatisfaction with the Wheat Board. It is also one more indication of the direction – and origin – of Tory policy. Again, at their Annual meeting in 1989, the Sask Pool delegates stated their position clearly:

> Quota levels and enforcement procedures must give all producers an equal opportunity to deliver to the elevator of their choice, and interest free cash advances must be available to producers to facilitate the orderly movement of grain.

Finally, in the same policy paper, the Pool delegates pointed out that "The Canadian Wheat Board is neither a subsidized entity, nor is it trade distorting in its practices. The operating costs of the board are borne by producers, while its sales are made at world prices without the benefit of export subsidies."

National Grains Bureau

In 1986 the Tory government established the Grains and Oilseeds Branch in Agriculture Canada to consolidate the federal government's activities in this sector. At the same time, it transferred the Grain Marketing Bureau from External Affairs to the

Grains and Oilseeds Branch. Then it put this branch directly under a Minister of State for Grains and Oilseeds, giving the federal cabinet a direct hand in the affairs of this crucial sector of Canadian agriculture.

To round out this structure of control the National Grains Bureau was launched in Winnipeg in April, 1988, as a unit of Agriculture Canada under an assistant deputy minister who reports to the associate deputy ministry who reports to the Minister of State.* Grains and Oilseeds Minister Mayer described the function of the new agency as coordinating the development of long-term grains and oilseeds policies between government and industry. At the same time Mayer announced the formation of Grains 2000, a program designed to foster more industry involvement in policy development.[13] Among those to welcome the announcement was the Western Canadian Wheat Growers Association.

Palliser/Western Canadian Wheat Growers Association

The "traditional" view of government activity is that government becomes involved to serve the public interest and increase public welfare. The alternative view, according to a paper written for the Economic Council of Canada, is that "government intervention is in response to political pressure by individuals or groups." This activity is called "rent seeking," and is described in these terms:

> Individuals or groups with common interests (i.e., interest groups) lobby politicians for regulations and programs that are favourable to them. In exchange for such regulations, the interest groups provide the government with support . . . and legitimacy (i.e., the government can point to a large group that agrees with what the government is doing).[14]

There is no group in Canadian agriculture that better represents this "rent seeking" activity than Western Canadian Wheat Growers, which began as the Palliser Triangle Wheat Growers' Association, unless it is the Ontario Corn Producers' Association. The Canadian Cattlemen's Association probably now ranks third.

---

* In order of ascendancy, these were Dennis Stephens, Harold Bjarnason, and Charlie Mayer at the beginning of 1990.

(The CCA offers a recent example of just how well the rent seeking posture can work: early in 1990 its executive vice-president, and spokesman since 1970, went on to his reward as an advocate of "free trade" and the Market Economy with a Cabinet appointment to the Canadian International Trade Tribunal.)

> The specialist producer groups are less likely to emphasize the problems that Canadian farmers have in common and more likely to focus on the uniqueness of the commodity sectors. Indeed, in their belief that agriculture is a business (like any other), where efficiency is fostered and rewarded by the market economy, groups like the Canadian Cattlemen's Association and the Palliser Wheat Growers Association find closer identity of interest with agri-business – with processors, distributors, and retailers – than with the many farmers who judge the market economy to be unjust in its treatment of producers.[15]

The Palliser Triangle Wheat Growers' Association was formed in 1969-70, supported publicly by Otto Lang, MP, minister responsible for the Wheat Board in the Liberal Government of the time. Lang also established a Grains Group of industry representatives.[16] (After his electoral defeat in 1979, Otto Lang became a vice president of Pioneer Grain.)

> Palliser members adopted the farmer-businessman perspective in their policies and programs. Their president from 1970-74 was a farm machinery dealer and a governor of the Winnipeg Commodity Exchange as well as a farm owner. . . Palliser members channelled investment capital off the farm into corporation shares, and companies reciprocated by taking out Associate memberships. The Associate status of $300 per member was made available to any non-farm corporation.[17]

Speaking to the Western Canadian Wheat Growers in December, 1989, Lang, who had worked all through his term in the federal Liberal cabinet (1968-1979) to destroy the Wheat Board, predicted the demise of the Canadian Wheat Board by 2010 along with the disappearance of the supply management marketing boards, such as in dairy, poultry and eggs.* In an editorial comment on Mr. Lang's scenario, the *Manitoba Co-operator* pointed out that the Wheat Board "can't function if giant multinationals

---

* This was the same Liberal government that had Eugene Whelan, as Minister of Agriculture, strongly supporting marketing boards.

are given access to Prairie grain. . . The issue is whether we maintain a large and diversified export market, which can be kept only through the Board, or whether we become a residual supplier to the U.S. and the world. . ."[18]

In 1985 it was decided that the Palliser group, with its 2000 members, should take advantage of the hospitable environment provided by the new Conservative government to play a greater role in the determination of agricultural policy. They changed their name to the Western Canadian Wheat Growers Association, and then in March, 1986, began a major membership campaign with the aim of recruiting 13,000 new members by the end of the year. Under the leadership of executive director Barbara Isman (who later became director of corporate relations for Cargill Ltd.), they hired a professional agency to put 20 commission agents in the field to sell $100/year memberships door to door. (A 1989 WCWGA publicity brochure describes these commission agents – the term used by their president in an interview – as "member relations consultants".) By the end of 1987, they had achieved a membership of 12,000, along with a deficit of $211,000.[19] They became one of the Tory government's favourite farm lobby groups, even though their membership apparently stabilized at the rather low figure of 11,000 compared to the 60-65,000 members of, for example, the Saskatchewan Wheat Pool. According to the National Grains Bureau, more than 105,000 Canadian producers claimed grains and oilseeds as their main source of income in 1986. Of this total, there were 226 in Atlantic Canada, 3,139 in Quebec, 14,426 in Ontario and 87,661 in Western Canada.[20]

A 1986 promotional booklet published by WCWGA refers to the 1985 meeting and suggests that "The dollars and sense policies of the Wheat Growers are most attractive when survival holds a higher priority than ideology". The president's opening message concludes by warning against relinquishing opportunities "to those who are not actively farming, or believe it to be a social occupation." What is meant by this innuendo is clarified on the same and following pages where the WCWGA is referred to as an organization for "progressive business-minded farmers" and expresses a "need for a farmer organization which is responsible, represents the interests of practical farm business people and which will have influence in government decision making."

Despite the ideological burden of this language, WCWGA claims it eschews ideology.

Although the WCWGA claims to be "the largest and fastest growing voluntary farm group", the same document gives a most confusing picture, inviting the interpretation that they are receiving financial support from sources other than individual farmer members:

> Two years ago, the cost to service each member was slightly over $100.00. Although that figure had never technically been assessed by anyone, it did reflect the actual cost to the association, and our member reps were suggesting $100 as an appropriate amount... The actual cost is currently in the $95 range. Having implemented a variable rate fee, however, means that farmers are able to contribute over and above operating cost at their discretion... The association has conducted research projects for different government bodies in the past. These revenues have been derived from specific projects undertaken by the association:
> - Intensive cereal management
> - The evaluation of summerfallow practices
> - The evaluation of winter wheat producers in Saskatchewan [21]

Scanning the magazine of WCWGA quickly indicates the individualistic orientation of the group:"Given a fair opportunity, farmers will make rational business decisions geared to maximizing their profits. If organizing their own product marketing and transportation will provide a better return on their investment, most farmers will choose to do so."[22]

This "look out for number one" approach does not sound like the voice of the many farmers I have listened to across Canada. This is not just my own impression; it is corroborated by the findings of a Decima Research study carried out in 1989 for Prairie Pools Inc.[23] after Grains and Oilseeds Minister Mayer announced that he was removing oats from Wheat Board jurisdiction. WCWGA president Harvey McEwan wrote in his 1989 Report to Members:

> In early January, Grains and Oilseeds Minister Charles Mayer announced that oats marketing would be handled by the private trade effective August first, 1989. The WCWGA joined with other western farm organizations to applaud the government's decision. When the debate over oats became emotional and clouded by political rhetoric, the WCWGA responded with reasoned and balanced commentary on the benefits of the decision for western oats producers.

The WCWGA's "reasoned and balanced commentary" was apparently lost on the majority of prairie farmers. According to the Decima Research study, a substantial majority (63%) of western farmers disapproved of the federal government's decision to remove oats from Wheat Board jurisdiction.

> Cross tabular analysis reveals that "oats farmers" (69%) oppose the government decision . . . significantly more than do "non-oats farmers" (56%) . . . it is interesting that a majority of those farmers who do not grow oats also disapprove of the government action . . . It would appear that these farmers recognize that the removal of oats represents a larger issue and that there are implications for the on-going viability of the Canadian Wheat Board.[24]

In this context, it is interesting to go back to the 1984 Progressive Conservative party platform, in which it is proclaimed that "A P.C. Government will respect any decision made by the producers."[25] One way around such a principle, of course, is either not to consult farmers at all, or to consult only those who you know will agree with your policy. The Decima Research study referred to above found that "Fully 76% of respondents believe that the government undertook inadequate consultation with farmers before it made its decision to remove oats." [26]

This same study also ascertained that "overall, the provincial pools are identified as the most credible organizations for farmers in the prairies. These data indicate that the provincial wheat pools are seen to be providing an important service to western farmers and are an effective representative of farmers' concerns with the federal government."[27]

What is ironic in the whole study is the conclusion drawn about the strength of the pools as lobbyists for prairie farmers:

> Given the importance of a united and consistent voice in government relations and communications activity, the provincial pools are most likely to represent the interests of the greatest number of farmers and *the most likely to receive the attention of the federal government* (emphasis added).[28]

Such a conclusion may be the appropriate one given the data, but given the policy changes pursued by the federal government, the conclusion is obviously the wrong one. The "rent seekers" with the proper right-wing ideology are more likely to receive the attention of the federal government, regardless of their representational strength.

Wheat Marketing in Ontario

Outside of the prairie (great plains) area under the jurisdiction of the Canadian Wheat Board, southwestern Ontario is the most significant grain producing area in Canada. All sales of Ontario-grown wheat are handled by the Ontario Wheat Producers' Marketing Board which was established in 1958. Its powers are more limited than those of the Canadian Wheat Board.

The Ontario Wheat Marketing Board has the authority to appoint agents of the Board (elevators) and to set service fees and selling prices for wheat. There are no delivery quotas in Ontario as there are in the territory under CWB jurisdiction. The Ontario Wheat Producers' Marketing Board also has the authority to pool all producers' wheat and to make initial, interim and final payments to producers for wheat sold.

Export sales are made through multi-national grain companies by cargo lots on a bid basis, while domestic sales for human consumption are made directly by the Ontario Board.

Until 1988 the two-price system for wheat for domestic human consumption and wheat for export applied in Ontario as well as the Prairies. Beginning in 1990, the price for Ontario domestic milling wheat will be set on the basis of the daily Chicago Board of Trade price. This means that purchasers of Canadian wheat for milling in North America will be paying the same price regardless of source, at least in theory. This should suit the purposes of the multinational traders quite well, since it effectively puts the domestic milling wheat trade in their hands. At the same time it undercuts the principle of equity embedded in the marketing board concept and thus the strength of the Canadian Wheat Board itself.

Saskatchewan: Pool elevator faces Cargill's

CHAPTER 3

PEER PRESSURE

Cargill is the largest of the five private grain companies that dominate global grain trade. Number two globally is Continental (U.S.A.), followed by Dreyfus (France), Andre/Garnac (Switzerland), and Bunge and Born (Brazil). Lately they have been joined by a sixth company, publicly held Mitsui/Cook (Japan – created when Mitsui outbid Pillsbury for the bankrupt Cook Industries Inc. in 1978). To indicate the measure of dominance of these companies, which might be described as a *sustainable oligopoly*: together these six companies account for some 95% of US wheat and corn exports, and the U.S. is the world's leading grain exporter.

What I mean by the term "sustainable oligopoly" is that there seems to be a certain stability, as well as regulatory and public acceptance, of this level of corporate concentration. The magic number, at least at present, appears to be five to seven corporations: in virtually every sector of the food system there are five to seven corporations that dominate, with one being the significant leader. In the grain trade this leader is Cargill. Similar oligopolies can be found in agricultural chemicals, seeds, food processing, food distribution, as well as in other sectors of the economy as a whole. It is likely that the number of firms that constitute a sustainable oligopoly at this time will drop once the public and the regulatory agencies get accustomed to the current level.

In Canada, Cargill is by far the most significant private trader and since early in 1988 Cargill has become a major, if not the major force, in Ontario agribusiness. A number of strategies have been undertaken recently by some of the other actors in the Canadian grain trade, perhaps to counter Cargill's development in Ontario and its growing national strength.

In November 1989, United Grain Growers formed a joint venture with Continental Grain. Canagrain International, as the new company is called, provides UGG with a global marketing structure while it gives Continental the ability to directly source Canadian grain for export. UGG handles about 18% of Prairie grains and Continental operates in 58 countries.

In 1987 United Cooperatives of Ontario leased its Windsor, Ontario, terminal to Archer Daniels Midland, a major U.S. soybean processor, established in 1912, which already owned the soybean processing plant next door (purchased by ADM from Maple Leaf Mills).*

In late 1989 UCO formed another association with ADM (ADM-UCO Grainco) whereby all grain delivered by its farmer-members to UCO elevators – mostly corn and soybeans – becomes, in effect, the property of ADM, which pays a per bushel fee to UCO and then markets the grain. This does not apply to wheat, which is under the jurisdiction of the Ontario Wheat Marketing Board.[29]

The aggressive Australian agri-business company Elders (Fosters Beer) has also been present in eastern Ontario with its big transfer terminal at Prescott, leased from the Federal Government. Elders became a highly visible buyer of specialty crops, including organically-grown crops, in both Ontario and the Prairies. One of its staff told me that 1989

---

* For the fiscal year ending June 30, 1989, according to its Annual Report, Archer Daniels Midland Company had "sales and other operating income" of $7.9-billion. For comparison, ConAgra, a fast-growing U.S. public agriculture and food conglomerate, had sales of $11.3-billion for the year ending May, 1989, according to its Annual Report.

was not a good year for Elders, and in March 1990 Elders announced it was selling all its grain elevators around the world.

In addressing the annual meeting of Saskatchewan Wheat Pool in 1989, the editor-in-chief of Milling and Baking News, the weekly journal of the "breadstuffs" industry, described "the great consolidation of the 1980s, which literally has occurred in every part of the world..."

> One consequence of great importance to you is the degree to which companies that are not farmer cooperatives have seized the opportunities offered by consolidation to strengthen their position in the origination of grain . . . I would guess that farmer cooperatives in the United States have gone from accounting for 60% of the grain origination to around 40% at the end of the 80s. [30]

In Canada, the co-ops (the three Pools plus UGG) accounted for 81% of grain origination in 1977, but this had dropped to 75% by 1987.

Cargill, in Canada as in the U.S., is a private corporation; its shares are not publicly traded. Like other privately-held corporations, it is not required by government regulation to disclose anything about itself and its operations that it does not choose to. But Cargill has a special significance for Canada and the world because it has more than a century's worth of accumulated information, accumulated experience and accumulated capital to draw on. It is also significant because it is integrated and because it is genuinely global; this means that Cargill owes no loyalty to any government or any people anywhere in the world.

> The largest firms in the industry are in a position to dictate prices, to limit entry, and effectively to conceal their profit margins. The same group of firms is likewise able to pursue its own interests at the expense of producers from any single country and without regard to national concerns. [31]

Consequently, it is simply unrealistic for a Canadian farmer, or a corporation or co-operative, be it a mill, elevator, feed company, fertilizer company, meat packer, or grain buyer, to assume that they can compete directly against Cargill in the marketplace.

Cargill Ltd., Graham Avenue, Winnipeg

Chapter 4

LONG TERM, LONG VIEW

Private Ownership and Control

> Cargill is not spending millions [on a corporate advertising cam-
> paign] for the sake of ego. Like everything it does, this is part of a
> well-thought-out, long-range plan. Since the early 60s Cargill has
> become increasingly active in attempting to influence U.S. grain
> trade and farm policies.[32]

Flexibility and the long view are key to any understanding of
Cargill Inc. and its development. Taking advantage of the chau-
vinism that confines the thinking of many others to national limits, Cargill has utilized brains, technology, and information from
around the world to chart its own course. Political boundaries are
not apt to limit either its imagination or the execution of its
plans.

Cargill is not an exception, or a bad example. Cargill is, in
fact, simply doing what corporations are supposed to do. A corporation is, after all, a legal persona created in order to take advantages of the rights and privileges accorded a person in some soci-
eties – with the distinct advantage over mere human beings that

it need not grow old and die and does not have a conscience. It can concentrate on the pursuit of growth and power without restraint.* To be employed by such an eternal persona may well imbue a person with a sense of security and even transcendence, particularly if one believes in making money as the basic ethic. And for those at the top there is unassailable control, and wealth.

> According to *Forbes* magazine, the less than 500 owners of Cargill – fewer than 50 are descendants of the company founders and the rest are current members of management – hold $2.6-billion in shareholder equity and get about $10 million a year in dividends. Four Cargill heirs were listed among the 400 richest people in the U.S. by *Forbes*, each with more than one-quarter of a billion dollars: James Cargill, [age] 64; W. Duncan MacMillan, 57; Whitney MacMillan, 58; Cargill MacMillan Jr., 60. [33]
>
> In 1989, *Forbes*, in their listing of "the 400 richest people in America", cited Whitney MacMillan, age 64, chief executive officer of Cargill, Inc., as holding 25% of Cargill stock valued at "at least $1.4-billion", while W. Duncan MacMillan, John Hugh MacMillan and Marian MacMillan Pictet between them hold another 25% of Cargill stock at a similar value. [34]
>
> [*Forbes* may be able to explain the discrepancies.]

As a private company with a very limited number of family and senior management shareholders, Cargill has never had to worry about the short-term demands of the capital market or the prying eyes of investors. With the owners being so few in number and so wealthy, there is little reason for them to make demands on the resources of the corporation. As a consequence, with the

---

* As described above, a corporation is a legal persona with the potential of immortality and a drive to *own* – as private property – the means of its survival. Recent developments in biotechnology and genetic engineering, accompanied by the move to extend "intellectual property rights" to life itself through redefinition of patents, are an expression of this "survival instinct". Private corporations like Cargill are like Harvard University's patented mouse (a genetically engineered mouse containing a patented gene). They are life forms, living organisms, privately owned.

odd bond issue, an open line of credit with its bankers and immense internal capital resources, Cargill has the financial ability to buy, move, or sell when it deems it to be in its own best interest. It need not have, and consequently does not have, any loyalties other than to its own corporate welfare.

With the benefit of freedom from public scrutiny and the sovereignty that its status as a transnational corporation provides, Cargill can buy commodities or facilities in a depressed market, or it can acquire apparently run-down properties for which it sees a long-term purpose, knowing that it has the resources to wait it out. (This is, after all, how the really wealthy survived the Great Depression or the crash of '87.) In some cases a site for an elevator may be worth more to Cargill than any standing facility on that property, such as the Cyanamid location in Alliston, Ontario, acquired in 1989; the ability to buy its way into a market or a region may set the price. Because of its structure, a company like Cargill may also spread a liability or a risk not only among a number of subsidiaries, but even among a number of countries. Who beyond the boardroom is to know if Cargill paid too much or is taking a loss on a particular operation for a few years?

> Through its management philosophy and its business investments, Cargill is dedicated to sound and prosperous Canadian agricultural industry.[35]

Cargill makes a practice, if not an art, of parading its commitment to Canada's national welfare, or the welfare of its agricultural sector, but one must remember that Cargill will say the same thing in every other country in which it operates. It might not be too crude to suggest that the "sound and prosperous agricultural industry" that Cargill refers to is itself.

Cargill's structure

Because it is a private company, it is virtually impossible to produce an accurate account of Cargill's business activities and its structure. The prospectus it published in 1987 is a rare document, and it has been reported that Cargill was unhappy to have to disclose even the meagre amount of information this prospectus made available to the public, and regretted having made the decision to go to the public bond market at all.

That prospectus did provide the following information about Cargill's activities and structure:

> The company's largest and most important businesses continue to be grain and commodity marketing, and vegetable oilseed and corn processing and refining. . .
>
> Cargill is organized into several principal operating areas:
>
> The Commodity and Trading Groups are responsible for grain and commodity origination and merchandising, including hedging, as well as merchandising of coffee, cocoa, wool, rubber, sugar, molasses, cotton, metals, ores, concentrates, petrochemicals, petroleum products and crude oil on a worldwide basis. . .
>
> The Processing and Milling Groups are responsible for. . . oilseed processing, milling and fruit processing activities. . .
>
> The Company and its subsidiaries have various lawsuits, arbitrations and actions pending against them, including but not limited to civil antitrust litigation. . . alleged breach of contract. . . damages. . . also involved in or subject to various antitrust, tax and other governmental investigations. . . In the opinion of management, any ultimate liability in these matters will not be material in relation to the consolidated financial position of the Company.[36]

Cargill's International Structure and Finances

Cargill established its corporate trading company, Tradax, in Panama in 1954, but as *Business Week* reported in 1979, this is merely a "letter box" tax shelter. Owned 70% by Cargill and 30% by a consortium of Swiss banks, the functional headquarters of Tradax has always been in Geneva, Switzerland. Panama, of course, provides a certain anonymity plus tax advantages for financial operations, while Geneva provides excellent communications and transportation for a global corporation.

The Tradax system has other advantages: when Cargill obtains an order for grain for delivery at some future date (an optional-source contract), it can shop around the world for the least-cost supplier and perhaps buy and sell that grain contract several times over before actually taking delivery of any real grain or delivering it to the customer. It might even trade that paper grain several times between various Tradax subsidiaries. In addition to the profit-taking opportunities such activities provide, they also have the advantage of obscuring Cargill's trading activities from both its competitors and government regulatory or reporting agencies. As a Dreyfus executive put it, Cargill is certainly number one, but by how much is a good question since one never knows how many times the same shipment of grain has been counted as it moves through the Cargill system.

The infrastructure required for day to day operations is provided by Cargill Financial Services (which functions as Cargill's own private bank), Tradax, Cargill Investor Services, Inc. (with offices in Chicago, Minneapolis, New York, Atlanta, Coral Gables, and Kansas City, as well as in Geneva, Zurich, London and Tokyo), and Cargill's global network of other facilities. By shifting expenses and profits from place to place, Cargill can mystify even the best government auditors. What is given as Cargill's sales or profits for any one aspect of its business, or any national unit, like Cargill Ltd. of Winnipeg, are what Cargill chooses to allocate to those categories for its own purposes. If there is a tax advantage in showing a loss somewhere, that can easily be arranged. By the same token, profits can be siphoned off through Tradax in Panama sight unseen, or made to appear to suit corporate plans. (This structure works well for other private corporations as well, of course.)

The result is some interesting figures in financial statements.[37] *(see table)* The figures are for Cargill Inc.'s wholly owned Canadian subsidiary, Cargill Ltd.

These figures appear to make some sense in relationship to each other except for the last line. Recognizing that there are no figures given for sales volumes, and that grain prices are unstable, there is still no obvious reason why net income figures vary so. Perhaps it is all in how the books are kept after all.

In the same non-consolidated financial statement cited above there are some other interesting figures pertaining to corporate income taxes *(see table)*. According to these figures, Cargill paid no tax in 1988 but $2.5-million in its fiscal year 1989.

Year ended 5/31/– (thousands of $)	1989	1988	1987	1986	1985	1984
Receivables	131,734	113,359	81,253	71,004	65,333	59,930
Payable	159,403	138,395	92,896	111,942	106,513	123,349
Sales	1,463,392	1,111,000	1,114,008	1,201,473	1,556,782	1,656,770
Net income	15,272	1,896	10,376	NA	NA	NA

Cargill coporate income taxes [figures indicated (---) are negative]

	1989	1988
Current Income Taxes	$(1,565,900)	(2,525,100)
Deferred Taxes	4,116,000	1,760,000
Net	2,550,100	(765,100)

The same statement explains: *The effective rate of tax is different from the statutory income tax rate of 44% for the following reasons:*

	1989	1988
statutory rate	44.0%	48.5%
investment tax credit	(1.4)	(25.3)
taxable capital gains	(.3)	(37.9)
non-taxable dividends	(24.3)	(18.2)
Prince Rupert tax allocation	(5.4)	(48.7)
other permanent differences	1.8	14.0
effective rate	14.4%	(67.6)

Source: Library of Parliament

While these figures, by themselves, do not tell any kind of whole story, they do indicate the reasons that Cargill paid no tax in 1988 and why their very low rate in 1989 still produced a tax bill, at least on paper, of $2.5-million as noted above. Will 1989 taxes be deferred and wiped out by a negative rate in 1990?

In this context, it is perfectly reasonable for Cargill's Canadian president, Kerry Hawkins, to say that Cargill Ltd. has never paid a dividend to its U.S. parent and that each year its cash flow is reinvested in Canada. [38] What to one accountant may appear as a "dividend" could just as easily appear to another as a "management fee" or an inflated price for goods or services, particularly if the accountant in question worked for the corporation being analyzed.

Since 1981, Cargill has reinvested 87% of its cash flow. Only 3% of the company's profits are paid out in dividends. Cargill also has an unusual habit of using its capital to expand or enter into depressed commodity businesses. Still another secret to Cargill's success is its global information system. . . [Cargill chairman] Mr. MacMillan said, "We don't look at what happens to our business in 6-month periods". Cargill officials focus on rolling five-year averages instead. [39]

Information systems

The perspective of Cargill's senior executives may be enriched by the location of its head office in a quasi-French 18th-Century country estate nestled amidst the woods and waters of Minnesota (west of Minneapolis). That reflective perspective is, however, also given leverage by means of Cargill's information system, which includes everything from satellite intelligence to on-the-ground evaluators.

Cargill, Inc., has announced plans to install a satellite-communications network that will link corporate headquarters here [Minneapolis] with the company's businesses at 250 locations in 40 states and "help serve rural customers more efficiently.". . . the network will replace Cargill's non-voice data-communications lines, including its leased teletype system . . . the network will transmit data from origin points to destinations in one-half second via a satellite located 22,300 miles over the equator. [40]

Cargill employees talk about *The Chateau* in hushed tones; for the majority of them, it is out of bounds. But its beauty and elegance are well known. The road to "the chateau" winds through the woods and along a lake in an idyllic setting. It curves around a gentle slope, and suddenly brings you to a mansion covered with vines. The grounds are exquisitely landscaped.

Inside, understated elegance envelopes the visitor. The entire building has been painstakingly renovated and furnished with superbly tasteful furniture, authentic antiques, oriental carpets, fine artwork. The only indicator that this is an office rather than a residence is that to the right of the softly lit, classically furnished entrance hall, is the "war room", with rows of computers and large clocks showing the time across the world. Men in three-piece suits intently watch computer screens and earnestly speak on phones making and breaking fortunes. These are Cargill's top buyers and sellers.

But there's a stillness and a hush in the chateau. Occasionally an elegant executive secretary tiptoes down the grand stairway and disappears behind a polished oak archway. Upstairs, the door of the boardroom is ajar . . . but there is no office furniture there either: plush armchairs in a circle with a small coffee table beside each. It's part of Cargill's Japanese-style management: to encourage the flexibility and creativity of its most-high-powered brains, Cargill offers them beauty and comfort. – *a visitor*

That such a communications system could also connect Cargill's brokers and trading offices around the world hardly needs to be suggested, though Cargill advertises it only obliquely. A two page ad in *Milling and Baking News*[41] delivered this message:

This ad is not about how hard we work. Everybody works hard. But it is about how hard we work to understand the world grain market. That's why we have our own meteorologists who get their information straight from the satellites. And can probably tell you more about world-wide weather patterns than your evening weatherman. That's why we have our crop forecasters who spend the bulk of their time on the road, checking crops. Sometimes before even the independent surveyors do. And that's why we have our own research librarians who can access 600 different data bases and have records dating back to who knows when. (Sorry, only Cargill employees can use them.)

Financial management

In the fall of 1989 Cargill started aggressively advertising its role in providing financial services to the grain industry and its use of the futures market, particularly the Chicago Board of Trade. With probably the most sophisticated crop intelligence gathering network in the world, from infra-red satellite photographs of grain-growing areas around the world to corporate staff in every grain producing and trading centre, Cargill has positioned itself to take advantage of every trading opportunity, whether that be in the purchase or sale of real grain or the trading of paper grain and other commodities.

Cargill's financial management is conservative, however, and the company tends to shy away from more speculative activities in favour of *hedging*, which it defines as "the process of transferring price risk from someone who does not want such risk to someone willing to accept it."[42]

> Every time it buys a commodity, it hedges by selling a contract to offer a like amount at some future time. When it sells the commodity, it buys the futures contract back. It is a highly conservative and safe approach from which Cargill never strays. [43]

To translate this into common language, Cargill prefers to make its money not in speculating, but in putting huge amounts of any given commodity through its system, where it can collect charges and fees for handling, storage and transport as well as making small margins on the trades themselves. To minimize the risk inherent in dealing in different currencies and other unforeseen risks like wars and weather – events over which it has not managed to gain control, that is – Cargill engages in what the trade calls *hedging*. Thus when Cargill buys a carload of real barley at price x, it sells a contract to deliver a like amount of barley at the same, or slightly higher, price at a specified future date. Whatever the fate of the real barley, Cargill knows that it can actually sell that amount of barley at a known price in the future. If, in the meanwhile, it can get a higher price for the real barley, it will sell it, perhaps at the same time redeeming (calling for delivery on) another futures contract that it had purchased earlier.

For example, if Cargill decides to sell oats that it has in storage to Saudi Arabia because the price is right or the U.S. Government is offering a subsidy, then at the same time it will buy a contract to take delivery of a similar amount of oats (possibly in Canada) at a future date for a price that balances, more or less, the sale just made.

Cargill's own monthly publication, *Cargill Bulletin*, frequently carries articles extolling the merits of the futures market and hedging. In promoting its services to farmers, helping farmers hedge their own grain sales ranks high on Cargill's list:

> When it comes to marketing your crop, you can count on Cargill's experience to help you get the best return ... We offer flexible grain marketing alternatives to reduce price risk and boost profits. If you prefer, we can store your crop to help reduce your on-farm investment, and position your grain for sale.[44]

One should not confuse Cargill's fiscal conservatism with its function as a trader: it is Cargill's task to make money coming and going, that is, buying as well as selling. Of course, Cargill also stands to gain in advising farmers to hedge their own crops, since it may well be Cargill that provides the brokerage service, for a fee or a percentage. Thus the grain company ends up, if it does its job well, storing the farmer's grain, brokering the grain and probably buying the grain and making money on the sale of the grain itself. This is not to mention the "crop inputs" that Cargill also supplies: fertilizer, chemicals and seeds. The profit opportunities would seem to be boundless, if prudently taken in small increments.

Nevertheless, Cargill insists on its corporate dedication to service. In the words of Whitney MacMillan:

> We believe we can contribute to rural development by investing in the services necessary for successful agricultural production. Providing seeds, feeds, fertilizer, storage, distribution and marketing services are obvious and important examples. We also could be a source of production credit, farm implements, harvesting services and insurance. And we can offer plenty of plain old good advice accumulated from our worldwide experience. [45]

The good advice, of course, reflects a particular perspective which is brought to bear on public policy as well as on the individual farmer.

Chapter 5

RIDING THE GRAVY TRAIN

Cargill, Inc. was established about 1865 by Will Cargill in the U.S. upper mid-west. With his two brothers he rapidly bought and built grain silos and elevators as the railway network expanded. Rapid expansion coupled with speculation in both elevators and grain brought the company close to bankruptcy in 1909 but it was salvaged by the MacMillans who had married into the Cargill family in 1895. By 1920 the family business was on the road to global expansion.

Post-World War II grain aid to Europe through the U.N. Relief and Rehabilitation Agency, and then the Marshall Plan of the United States, made a significant contribution to Cargill's fortunes. U.S. wheat and flour exports jumped from 48 million bushels in 1944 to 503 million in 1948.

U.S. grain exports dropped as Europe recovered, but went up again with Public Law 480 (often known as "Food For Peace"), introduced in 1954. By the 1950s the European view of the dumping of U.S. grain in Europe was no longer one of welcome aid but of threatening competition. The Europeans were determined to become self-sufficient in food production to the greatest extent possible after their experience of food insecurity during the war years. The response of American agribusinesses and farm interests was an ingenious plan which became Public Law 480.

Under PL480 the US continued to ship farm surpluses abroad but directed them primarily to underdeveloped countries that could not afford to pay with dollars . . . With local currency received as payment from recipient governments, the US government covered expenses for military security, embassy costs, and the purchase of strategic materials. . .

The program had the immediate strategic advantage of tying developing nations more closely to US interests.

The link between government food aid during the 50s and 60s and current levels of commercial exports to key countries is striking. [46]

Cargill, acting as an agent for the government, has always been one of the prime beneficiaries of PL480 financing. At the same time Cargill has benefitted as a private trader as those Food For Peace grain exports "whetted the appetites" of many new potential customers for subsequent commercial sales. In fact, the promise of eventual commercial purchases was often a specific precondition for the food aid in the first place. Food aid, particularly wheat, was utilized very much like infant formula: to create a taste, and a market, for a company's products for a lifetime.

Between 1955-65, Cargill's U.S. grain exports increased 400%, with sales rising from $800-million to $2-billion. By 1963 Public Law 480 had generated sales for Cargill and Continental of $1-billion each. (This was for storing and transportation, primarily, not for processing or manufacturing.) In addition to its increased sales, Cargill also benefitted from the government's grain storage program. Between 1958-68 it received some $76-million for storing grain, often in leased publicly-owned terminals or terminals built with public funds. Cargill's reputation in the trade for manipulating government programs to its advantage is extensive.

U.S. policy shifted in 1964 from subsidizing the storage of grain to subsidizing grain exports. Export subsidies then went to the grain companies so that they could discount the price and sell grain below the prevailing world market price. These subsidies meant that the government could reduce its grain storage costs while increasing foreign exchange earnings. Dan Morgan, in *Merchants of Grain*, points out that "Officially, this was called 'making American agricultural products more competitive abroad'."

At the height of U.S. "grain power" in the 1970s, companies like Cargill Ltd. and Continental Grain Co. made fortunes out of U.S. agricultural exports. Privately owned and secretive, they are the two largest members of a group of five companies that controls between 85 and 90% of U.S. grain exports, 80% of Argentina's wheat sales, and 90% of the cereals exported by the European Community . . . Fierce advocates of a free market for agriculture, they have become overwhelmingly dependent on Government efforts to increase their sales.[47]

There have been many publicly funded programs that have benefitted the "free enterprise" grain processors and merchants, like the Targeted Export Assistance Program allocation from the Foreign Agricultural Service of the U.S. Department of Agriculture. Assistance from these public programs is often channelled through non-profit foundations and associations so that corporate behaviour does not appear so unseemly. U.S. Wheat Associates and the U.S. Feed Grains Council are among 46 organizations that have received support from the Targeted Export Assistance Program, and U.S. Wheat Associates has been involved in several wheat foods product promotions. One such project sent 100-tonne samples of various U.S. wheat classes to mills around the world and U.S. specialists helped work with the potential foreign users. Mills in Senegal, Burkino Faso, Colombia, Taiwan, and many other markets have participated in this program. In 1988 more than 1000 small bakeries in Korea participated in this program and 10 new baked foods were introduced.[48]

In 1989, The National Association of Wheat Growers Foundation developed a project called "The Developing World: Opportunities for U.S. Agriculture". The intent is to increase opportunities for U.S. wheat exports to less developed countries. "The project will train up to 30 growers to make presentations to state and local groups, and through the media, on economic development and trade and *the potential of less developed countries to enhance the U.S. economy.*"[49] *(emphasis added)*

The Export Enhancement Program of the 1985 Food Security Act is the most notorious of the publicly funded corporate assistance programs, public rhetoric about its benefits to U.S. farmers notwithstanding. Clayton Yeutter, who at the time was U.S. Trade Representative, explained that such programs were necessary to counter the European Community and to subsidize

U.S. farmers so they could compete on world markets.[50] Because of the federally set target price and the federal loan rate on commodities, American farmers are isolated from so-called market prices; nevertheless, farmers nowhere benefit from the low price of wheat. It is the traders who receive the benefits. So while the U.S. government subsidizes the exporters, it also has to subsidize the farmers in order to keep them going.

Who really benefitted? By June 10, 1988, E.E.P. sales totalled $4.97-billion, with half of those sales to China and the U.S.S.R.[51] In 1988-89 the E.E.P. program nearly doubled. As reported in *Milling & Baking News*[52], "since May, 1985, there have been 104 export enhancement initiatives announced, targeting 65 countries and 12 commodities. Sales under E.E.P. have aggregated $8.5-billion with $2.57-billion in Commodity Credit Corp. stocks or payment-in-kind certificates as bonus rewards." In other words, while continuously condemning the "trade distorting practices" and the government involvement in the Canadian Wheat Board, Cargill is happy to cooperate with what has, in the United States, become a *de facto* state trading corporation.

In 1987 it was reported that wheat sales to China under the new E.E.P. netted Cargill bonuses worth $2-million, while Dreyfus and Continental each benefitted by half that amount.[53]

According to a Reuters dispatch,[54] under the U.S. Export Enhancement Program Cargill and Continental Grain have each received more than $400-million in public benefits, out of a total of more than $2.5-billion in export subsidies in four and a half years.

In case there was ever any doubt as to the intent of the Export Enhancement Program, the new guidelines developed in late 1989 make quite explicit who is to benefit. The U.S. Department of Agriculture grouped the guidelines into four areas. The first two of these are:

1 – *Trade Policy Effect*: E.E.P. proposals must further the U.S. negotiating strategy of countering competitors' subsidies and other unfair trade practices by displacing exports in targeted countries.

2 – *Export Effect*: All E.E.P. initiatives must demonstrate their potential to develop, expand or maintain markets for U.S. agricultural commodities.[55]

In its first year, the Export Enhancement Program accounted for only 12% of the 25 million tonnes of U.S. wheat exported, but by 1987-88 this had climbed to 70% of the 45 million tonnes exported. During this same period the debt of the Third World or "less developed" countries was growing and they were increasingly unable to afford the grains that the U.S. needed to sell. Since "The Market" was unable to play its part in moving U.S. grain surpluses, government intervention became a necessity. Somewhere along the way the "law of supply and demand" disappeared, but this does not seem to have offended the advocates of a market economy. Cargill, for one, seems to have had little trouble accessing the public subsidy network, ranging from the EEP (which may subsidize whole grains or milled flour and other "value-added" commodities), to storage fees or marketing assistance. Being vertically integrated and global in scope, Cargill has in fact been well disposed to take advantage of them all.

A small sample of Cargill's global directory
(2 of 8 pages– not including North America)

ARGENTINA

Buenos Aires: Cargill SACI
Carabassa:Cargill SACI Poultry Div.
Pergamino: Cargill SACI Seed Div.
Puerto San Martin: Cargill SACI
Quequen (Necochea):Cargill SACI

AUSTRALIA

Brisbane: Queensland
  Oilseed Crushers Pty. Ltd.
Fremantle: Cargill Wool Brokers
  Cargill Wool Pty. Ltd.
Melbourne: Cargill Australia Ltd.
  Cargill Oilseeds, Cargill Processing,
Cargill Wool Pty.
Narrabri: Cargill Oilseeds
  Cargill Processing
Perth, Western Australia
  Leslie Salt Co.
Port Hedland, W. Australia
  Leslie Salt Co.
Sydney: Cargill Wool Pty.
Toowoomba: Cargill Seeds

BARBADOES:

see West Indies

BELGIUM

Antwerp: N.V. Cargill
  Tennco Europe, S.A.
Ghent: Euro-Silo N.B.
  N.V. Cargill
Herent: Malteries Leon Dreyfus

BERMUDA

Hamilton: Cargill Export Ltd., Cargill
  Agricola, Marine Transportation
  Co., SPCL Ltd., Tennco
International
  Ltd., Tradax Petroleum Ltd.

BRAZIL

Andira: Sementes Cargill
Bebeduoro:Cargill Citrus Ltda.
Cameinas: Sementes Cargill
  (Research)
Feira de Santa: Marau S/A Agro
  Industria e Commercio
Ilheus: Cargill Cacau Ltd. (Plant)

Jose Bonifacio: Cargill Ag. (Excel)
Maringa: Cargill Agricola S.A.
  (Excel),
  (P/R), (Feed)
Marinque: Cargill Agricola S.A.
Monte Alto: Cargill Agricola S.A.
Paranagua: Cargill Ag. S.A. (Ports)
Ponta Grossa, Parana: Cargill Ag.
Rio de Janeiro: Cargill Ag.
Salvador: Cargill Cacau Ltda.
Santos: Cargill Ag.(Coffee Dept.),
  Santos Terminal (Citrus)
Sao Paulo: Cargill Ag. Head Office
Uberlandia: Cargill Agricola S.A.
Uchoa: Cargill Citrus Ltda.

CHILE

Santiago: Cargill Chile Ltda.

COLOMBIA

Bogota:Cargill Colombiana SA, Compania Cafetera de Manizales, Ltda.
Cali: Cargill Colombiana, SA

DOMINICAN REPUBLIC

Santo Domingo: Cargill Dominicana

ECUADOR

Quito: Cargill del Equador, SA

EL SALVADOR

San Salvador: Termicar SA, Alimentos de Animales, S.A., La Sultana,
S.A., Avinsa, S.A., Proveedora de
Granjaz, S.A.

ENGLAND

Avonmouth: Internat'l Molasses Ltd.
Blackburn: Redmayne&Isherwood
Ltd.
Bootle: Cargill UK Ltd., Commodity
  Marketing Div., Soybean
Processing
  Div.
Bradford: Cargill Wool Ltd.
Cambridge: Cargill UK Ltd.
Cargill Agricultural Merchants
Dereham: Shaver Poultry Breeding
  Farms (GB) Ltd.
Felixstowe: International Molasses. . .

Chapter 6

DEEP POCKETS

Cargill's global trading house, TRADAX, has a network of "independent" subsidiaries which gives it maximum flexibility in arranging – and obscuring – global transactions. For example, highly imaginative accounting is possible when Tradax purchases Thai tapioca (made from cassava) from Cargill Thailand for shipment to a Cargill subsidiary in Holland as a feed supplement for Dutch hogs. Or Cargill can get around U.S. requirements for disclosure of major grain sales by selling among its subsidiaries, with Tradax making the final sale. As Dan Morgan documented so thoroughly, any speculative activity is greatly facilitated when there is public secrecy and confusion. [56]

For decades Cargill has been able to count on the Chase Manhattan Bank to assist in meeting its cash requirements,[57] while at the same time Cargill's headquarters acts as a bank for its worldwide organization. As of Nov. 1977, Cargill had investments in and loans outstanding to subsidiaries and affiliates of more than $754-million. It was also using at least 43 banks with an *un*secured line of credit for at least $300 million. In 1978 it was reported that Cargill was able to arrange well over $1-billion in prime-rate domestic and foreign bank credit lines, including short-term credit used exclusively to finance its commodity inventories. [58]

Unity in Diversity

Cargill has used this financial clout to diversify both in terms of commodities and in terms of geography. For example, Cargill went into soybean crushing in 1945 while also buying Nutrena Mills in the U.S. In 1947 Cargill opened a $2-million grain storage and processing plant in Puerto Rico and in 1948 it moved into Brazil. In 1968 Cargill paid $68-million for MBPXL, now Excel, the second or third largest meat packer in the U.S. Caprock, its beef feeding company, is the largest feedlot operator in the U.S.

Between 1970-78 Cargill bought two steel companies, turkey processing and marketing facilities, flour companies, grain elevators in Canada, built plants to process high fructose corn syrup (HFCS), all for a total cost of some $300-million.

By the mid-'70s the U.N. listed Cargill as the twentieth largest food processing company in the world. It dominated soybeans globally as well as in the U.S., with 30% of the U.S. soybean crush in 1986. It has interests in other oilseeds as well, for example in France where "les Cargill-boys" engaged in a long struggle over the marketing of sunflowers in the late 1980s.[59]

In 1971-2 Cargill's earnings after taxes were $19.4-million. The next year they were $150-million. (The massive Soviet grain purchases made during this period are often referred to as "The Great Grain Robbery" though the term might be more aptly applied to the profits of the grain traders.)

Richard Gilmore, in *A Poor Harvest*, reported that in fiscal 1973 the sale of wheat to the Soviet Union in 1972 cost the U.S. $300-million in subsidies, most of which went to the largest private exporters. "The windfall came from the fact that several firms, having made sales to their foreign affiliates before the government's notice of the forthcoming termination of the subsidy program, subsequently registered these sales at the peak subsidy rates."[60]

The upheaval in the global grain market in the early '70s was matched in its profitability for the merchants of grain by the American embargo on grain sales to the U.S.S.R. in 1980. The following are two descriptions of the same events, the first from Cargill's *Bulletin*, the second from an American farm organization:

> As a result of the Soviet invasion of Afghanistan in 1979, the U.S. Govt. embargoed sales of agricultural goods to the Soviet Union. By the fall of 1980 . . . the government was in the process of assuming the contractual obligations for 13 million tons of corn and 4 million tons of wheat once destined for the Soviet Union. Eventually, most of the contracts were sold back into the marketplace. The embargoed wheat, however, was purchased outright and the 4 million tons were placed in reserve.[61]

> When the Carter administration imposed its embargo on the Soviet Union . . . the USDA compensated Cargill and its colleagues for grain they had agreed to, but could no longer, ship. A 1981 report by the Agriculture Department Inspector General . . . described possible manipulation by unnamed companies. Large amounts of grain were reclassified as bound for the Soviet Union and thus made eligible for compensation.[62]

In recent years, Cargill has moved rapidly into further processing of commodities, so that by 1986, "20% of all the commodities Cargill buys are now ultimately processed by Cargill factories, grain mills and oil presses."[63]

> U.S.-based Cargill Inc., one of the world's largest trading firms, is planning to revive its oil milling operations in the Philippines after five years of absence brought about by former President Marcos' policy of restricting investments in the industry. Cargill currently trades through its Philippines-based subsidiary, Agro-Tex Commodities Inc. . . . Cargill wants to set up an oil mill with a crushing capacity of at least 500 tonnes a day.[64]

In late 1989 Cargill was pushing, with the help of the U.S. government, for permission from the government of South Korea to build a soybean processing plant to produce edible oil. Both Commerce Secretary Mosbacher and Trade Commissioner Carla Hills pressed the Korean government to accept Cargill's proposal. A Korean newspaper reported that Korean soybean producers held less than 60% of the domestic market: "if Cargill expands here, it won't be just a matter of the sale of a few more bags of fodder or tanks of oil. That is because we can see in this move the terrible plan to export raw materials as well as to process them here for profit, then ultimately to force the small Korean businesses into bankruptcy and take over the whole market."[65] Korea's Agriculture Minister Kim said he would not approve the investment by Cargill because he feared that it would devastate the nation's soybean-related industries and soybean farming.[66]

The extent of Cargill's global activities is also reflected in its activities in Thailand, where it is moving beyond the interests in cassava processing (tapioca) which have already been mentioned. While it has abandoned poultry breeding with the sale of Shaver Poultry, chicken production remains on Cargill's agenda. Sun Valley Thailand is a joint venture of Cargill and a Japanese company, Nippon Meat Packers, to produce, process and market chicken meat in Thailand. A breeding farm, hatchery, growing facilities, a feed mill and processing plant are being constructed. Cargill is to be responsible for the production and processing of the chickens which Nippon will market, mostly in Japan.[67]

These processing activities, and Cargill's capacity to meet short-term market opportunities, are supported by its estimated 7 million tons of storage space around the world.

Chapter 7

HISTORIC DEVELOPMENT

1928   Cargill started trading grain in Canada, with an office in Winnipeg.

1953   Kerr Gifford Co. of Vancouver was purchased, providing Cargill with its first terminal elevators in Canada.

> While visiting Cargill's Nutrena feed mill in Stockton, California, I noticed that the old weathered name on the silos was "Kerr Gifford". This Stockton mill draws grain from Idaho, Nebraska, Wyoming and Montana and serves the west coast – mostly dairy herds numbering 400-500 head – plus exporting to the South Pacific!

1959   St. Lawrence Seaway opened. Cargill opened Canada's largest grain transfer elevator at Baie Comeau, Quebec, at the mouth of the St. Lawrence River.

1961   Cargill formed Nipigon Transport in partnership with Hanna Mining of Cleveland. Four bulk tankers in use, hauling grain from Thunder Bay and other lake ports down the St. Lawrence to Baie Comeau, hauling iron ore on the trip back up the river. The Iron Ore Co. of Canada had its headquarters in Baie Comeau, with Brian Mulroney as president. (At that time, Hanna Mining had interests in the properties being mined by Iron Ore of Canada.[68] An ex-Cargill employee in Baie Comeau told me that he, along with the other Cargill people, used to play golf with Mulroney.)

1965-1988   Cargill had major or total control of Shaver Poultry, Cambridge, Ontario. (Shaver's hybrid poultry, according to Shaver, are responsible for one third of all white eggs produced *in the world*.)

1971   Cargill Inc. bought P.A.G. Seeds (Ill.) including Canadian sales. The P.A.G. name disappeared in 1988, replaced by Cargill Hybrid Seeds, which also became Canadian distributor for Asgrow seeds. Asgrow is a subsidiary of the American drug company Upjohn.

1974   Cargill Ltd. purchased National Grain, (286 elevators, including its Thunder Bay terminal, and five feed mills). It then introduced Nutrena (Cargill's trade name) feeds to Canada.

1976   Brian Yaworski noted that both Cargill and Continental were manoeuvering to open the Canadian grain trade to private companies.

According to a U.S. Senate investigator, "there is a sentiment within the grain community that Canada may go off the Wheat Board." Cargill is already laying plans for the end of government export controls: late in 1974 Cargill Grain purchased . . . National Agri-Services . . . Roger Murray, president of Cargill Ltd. said the purchase "places Cargill Grain in a unique position to plan efficient future expansion in the handling, processing and exporting of Canadian grain, oilseeds and feed stuffs."[69]

1976   Canada's first producer-owned inland terminal, at Weyburn, Sask., built with the encouragement of CWB Minister Otto Lang, signed an agreement with Cargill under which Cargill was to be selling agent for all of the terminal's grain. Also in 1976, Cargill opened its second inland terminal, this one at Rosetown, Saskatchewan.

1978   Cargill entered into Ontario agribusiness with the purchase of Urlin Grain Co., Talbotville, Ontario:

Cargill is gambling that Canada's desire to capitalize on the new opportunity in world grain trade will lead it to permit the big private companies to share in the more profitable trading function. "We're counting on the Canadian system moving more toward free markets," says W.B.Saunders, group vice-president.[70]

1981   Cargill built its seed corn processing and storage plant in Princeton, Ont.

1981   Panco Poultry, of Surrey, B.C., a division of Cargill Grain Co., was shut down after three years of Cargill operation. Panco was processing 27% of the chickens sold in B.C. and Cargill had just completed a $2-million modernization of the Panco plant. Cargill laid the blame for closing the plant on the failure of the B.C. Chicken Marketing Board to give it more birds. Cargill president Roger Murray was reported to have said that, "there is no longer a sufficient margin between what the grower requires and what the consumer is prepared to pay to cover the cost of processing." The Marketing Board said "the consumer will not pay more than $1.55-1.60/lb."[71]

Cargill abandoned plans for an oilseed crushing plant in Melfort, Sask., when the provincial government would not come through with a $2-million grant.[72] "A government investigation of the Cargill books indicated the company is prosperous enough to build the rapeseed crushing plant on its own."[73]

1982   Cargill handled 8% of Prairie grain. (The three Prairie Pools together controlled about 60% of the grain handling market in Canada.) With its Thunder Bay terminal and Baie Comeau transfer elevators, Cargill had become the leading private exporting agent for the Canadian Wheat Board.

1986   Cargill vice-president Dick Dawson: "We don't want to be a grain company, we want to be an agricultural corporation."[74]

During 1985-86 Cargill acquired Kola Feeds, near Brandon, Manitoba, and expanded fertilizer services by adding four small blending facilities, starting 11 others, and buying two fertilizer sales operations in Saskatchewan and Manitoba. Twenty-eight of Cargill's 127 elevator locations were also improved.[75]

1987   Southern Feeds Ltd., Lethbridge, Alberta, bought by Cargill. Southern was southern Alberta's first major feed mill when it was built in 1964. This purchase made Cargill the major feed supplier for the beef feedlot industry in southern Alberta and complemented the liquid/block feed supplement plant it already had in Lethbridge.

1987   Ayr Feed and Supply (Ayr, Ontario) purchased, Cargill's first move into the "retail" feed and farm supply business in Ontario.

1988   Cargill sold Shaver Poultry of Cambridge, Ontario, to the French company, *Institut de Sélection Animale* (ISA) (Merieux Group), that has the biggest share of the world's brown egg market. (In December, 1989, Merieux also succeeded in gaining control of Connaught BioSciences of Toronto.) According to the press release, "Cargill has concluded that poultry breeding is out of the mainstream of its integrated poultry operations. Cargill will concentrate future resources on live production, processing and marketing of poultry products. . . . It has major poultry production, processing and marketing operations in Argentina, Honduras, the United Kingdom and the United States."

1988   Maple Leaf Mills Grain Division purchased from Hillsdown Holdings of Britain in April, 1988, for about $40-million. Maple Leaf Mills handled about 10% of marketed Ontario grain (grain not utilized on-farm) through its 23 country elevators in southwestern Ontario and four grain terminals: Midland, Port McNicoll and Sarnia, Ontario, and Saint John, New Brunswick. This acquisition also made Cargill Canada's largest soybean handler.

Maple Leaf Mills Grain Division, which Cargill acquired, was only a small portion of Maple Leaf Mills Ltd. which had been purchased in Sept. 1987 by Hillsdown Holdings for $361 million from Canadian Pacific Ltd.

Cargill Ltd. reported a profit of $5.6-million for the year ended May 31, 1989, on sales of $1.5-billion. It also reported investing more than $70-million in Canada during the year.[76]

Cyanamid facility at Alliston, Ontario

A recent acquisition

Chapter 8

NUTS AND BOLTS

Fertilizer

In January, 1989, Cargill Ltd. announced that it had purchased the retail fertilizer distribution network of Cyanamid Canada, Ltd. in Ontario and Quebec, composed of 14 wholly-owned retail dealerships and eight associated joint venture partnerships. The largest joint venture, Burford Fertilizer, at first refused the deal, but by the end of the year the two men who had owned the other half had sold out to Cargill. Another, in Ceresdale, Ontario, declined to make its sale public.

Then in May Cargill announced that it would build one of the world's largest fertilizer plants at Belle Plaine, Saskatchewan, in partnership with the provincial government. The $350-million nitrogen fertilizer plant was expected to be operating by the spring of 1992. The province and Cargill formed Saferco Products Inc. to build and own the plant. According to Agriweek , "The province's investment is temporary: it intends by this October to re-sell its interest to private investors. Said to be a last-resort option is a sale of the province's shares, privatization-style, to the general public . . . Cargill will have exclusive marketing rights to the plant's production, which will be sold under Cargill's and private brand names in western Canada, Ontario, and the northern U.S. states."[77]

Curiously, Cargill received assurances of provincial government support that were considerably more substantial than had been sought by Saskatchewan Wheat Pool for a similar proposal, which the government had turned down. In addition, a small Alberta company, Canadian 88 Energy Corp., had put forward a proposal for a series of small nitrogen fertilizer plants in Saskatchewan, asking the provincial government for a low-interest loan of only some $10-million to build the first one at Rosetown, Saskatchewan.

Cargill said at the time that the Belle Plaine plant would supply the prairies, Ontario and Quebec, but there is no way that Canadian farmers could buy or use the amount of nitrogen fertilizer the proposed plant would produce. On the other hand, the Mississippi River is closer than Vancouver (and no mountains!), making it feasible for the plant to be a "world-class operation", as Barbara Isman described it to me. Belle Plaine is about 40 miles west of Regina, and just west of Belle Plaine a mainline railway branches off in a south-easterly direction through Weyburn and Estevan, Saskatchewan, and on to Minneapolis at the head of the Mississippi River, where Cargill Port is situated.

Isman also indicated that Cargill was going for a joint venture at Belle Plaine because then the public financial support could not be defined as a subsidy in the context of the Canada-U.S. trade agreement.

Natural gas, the feedstock for nitrogenous fertilizers, is readily available, quite literally, from the pipeline "at the door". The supplier is SaskPower, which describes itself as "a provincially owned Crown Corporation, established in 1949 to provide electricity and natural gas to the residents of Saskatchewan."[78]

In announcing and defending the project, the provincial government stated that negotiations had been going on for some time. Apparently, then, while SaskPower was making changes in its structure to accomodate the deregulation of natural gas, it was also negotiating with Cargill concerning the disposition of a very large volume of that gas. In fact, the plant will be the largest consumer of natural gas in the province.

SaskPower's 1988 Annual Report stated:

In 1987, deregulation of natural gas brought a whole new way of operating to SaskPower's Gas System. Customers can now buy gas directly from producers, while SaskPower continues its important role of transporting natural gas within Saskatchewan. Deregulation also opened up the export market. Gas deregulation began in 1985 with an agreement between the federal government and the gas-producing provinces . . . to change the tightly regulated system for selling natural gas . . . It paved the way for buyers and sellers to negotiate prices, and gave producers access to more market opportunities.

The concepts and language would, of course, apply equally well to wheat, but in this case it means that Cargill, or Saferco, can negotiate freely with the producers of natural gas over volumes, rates and conditions, just as Cargill would like to be able to do with grains.

Late in 1989 the Conservative provincial government backed away from its plans to privatize SaskPower altogether due to overwhelming public opposition.

At a time when there is growing concern, in the context of the Canada-U.S. trade deal, over unlimited sales of natural resources, such as gas, to the U.S.A., a fertilizer plant provides an efficient way for a private corporation to export as much natural gas as it can, but in the form of liquid and granular fertilizer. Public criticism can be stifled by saying that these are "value added" commodities. The plant is expected to produce 1500 tonnes of anhydrous ammonia and 2000 tonnes of granular urea per day.

Both anhydrous ammonia and granular urea can easily be transported in bulk, by rail, to Cargill Port in Minneapolis for further shipment by water anywhere in the world. The other interesting aspect of this operation is that urea is a source of protein for livestock feed and could be well utilized by Cargill's Nutrena feed division. This could also give Cargill some additional leverage in the soybean market, soybeans being the primary source of protein for livestock feed.

In spite of severe public criticism for its generosity towards Cargill, in February, 1990, the Saskatchewan Government announced, with Cargill, that construction of the now-$435-million project would begin in the spring. The construction contract has been awarded to a German management firm.[79]

The plans call for Cargill to own 50% of the operating company, Saferco Products Inc., created for the project, while the Saskatchewan government will hold 49% with the remaining 1% going to a financial institution. This arrangement means that Cargill will have effective control over Saferco.

While claiming that the project will not require any public subsidies, the provincial government has agreed to provide a loan guarantee for the $305-million required for construction. The remaining $130-million is to come from the equity shareholders. Thus for $65-million Cargill is getting a $435-million fertilizer plant. Cargill also has first refusal if the province decides to sell any portion of its share.

Saskatchewan is also the world's largest producer of potash, the second major fertilizer component, which is mined 200-250 km. north of Belle Plaine. In the fall of 1989 the Conservative government of Saskatchewan took a series of steps to privatize the publicly owned (Crown Corporation) Potash Corporation of Saskatchewan, which had made a profit of $106-million for the people of Saskatchewan in 1988.

> The leaflet promoting this "opportunity" proclaimed: "Potash Corporation of Saskatchewan is becoming a Saskatchewan public company. This means that you too can participate with the Province of Saskatchewan and other investors in strengthening the future of this world-class industry leader . . . How? By purchasing Potash Corporation of Saskatchewan Inc., Ownership Bonds."

Potash Corporation owns four of the province's 10 mines and controls half of the potash industry in the province. Given the record of the Devine government, there is good reason to suspect that conversations were going on, while Cargill and the provincial government were ostensibly negotiating the Belle Plaine deal, as to how Cargill might also gain effective control over, or at least unrestricted access to, these potash resources.

In the fall of 1989 the provincial government was busy promoting the sale of the Ownership Bonds to Saskatchewan residents who, as residents, had already been the owners of Potash

Corporation of Saskatchewan. The government hoped to raise $100-million through the sale of these convertible bonds. By November it had also sold more than $200-million worth of common shares in the new company in Canada, the United States and Europe.[80] Whether Cargill was the buyer of any of these was not stated.

The third major fertilizer component, phosphate, is not found in Canada, but in 1985 Cargill Inc. purchased the Gairdinier phosphate mine in Florida. Even though that plant has severe ecological, and hence legal, problems, Cargill certainly has the resources to correct them to the extent required to become acceptable. Cargill has thus achieved secure access to all three basic fertilizer components.

Cargill, apparently, has once again successfully implemented its basic business philosophy: obtain unrestricted access to cheap raw materials, handle them in bulk in huge volumes, add value to them along the way if possible and trade in them globally. In the case of fertilizer components there is the special advantage of Cargill's existing global distribution network.

Mills and Elevators

In July, 1989, Cargill announced that it had purchased Arkona Feed Mills Ltd. of Arkona, Ont. Cargill also announced that it will spend more than $1-million to upgrade the plant to serve Michigan as well as Ontario with its Nutrena feeds. The business was purchased from the Brown family.

In an interview, John Brown explained that with Cargill behind the business, it could serve its customers and the area better, with more resources – information, people – to draw on than they could ever dream of as an independent mill. Brown said he was concerned about apprehension in the community over the sale, but that it did not seem to materialize.

Arkona is an area of dairy, corn and beans, and Cargill's acquisition of a major mill in the area will not foster diversification or sustainability. It is interested in specialization, and the export terminal at Sarnia is within the 100 mile radius that the mill serves.

Cargill fertilizer

An Alberta feedlot

A Cargill official also told me that if there are not enough feed materials – corn and soybeans – available in Ontario, it would still be reasonable to import from Michigan and Illinois and re-export the finished feed.

This move can be seen as part of a continental strategy when it is compared to another recent Cargill acquisition, this one in the U.S. In August, 1989, Cargill's Nutrena Feed Division purchased the major assets of Hansen and Peterson, Inc., near Burlington, Washington state.

> Cargill Nutrena . . . is a full-line producer with 58 mills in Canada and the U.S. The company operates Beacon Milling in the East and ACCO Feeds in the Southwest. [Acquisition of the Hansen and Peterson plant] represents its first foray into the Northwest [and] moves Nutrena closer to its "feed distribution goals" to be a national feed manufacturer. In building its national system, Nutrena acquired Beacon four years ago and bought ACCO from Quaker Oats two years ago . . . The area served by the Hansen and Peterson plant is the country's dairy showcase.[81]

This new acquisition will complement the Nutrena mill in Stockton, California, giving Cargill thorough coverage on the West Coast. This also suggests that Cargill is convinced that the dairy and cattle business will continue to concentrate in the West.

Meat

> Canada should get into the meat business, as well as grain, according to Cargill senior vice-president Dick Dawson. "More people all over the world are living better today. Our challenge is to grow more tons, value add to more meat, value add again to more further processing and selling into a rising market. . . More people live at even higher standards the world over. More people also starve. All the graphs point upward. We are in an irreplaceable business on a growth trend."[82]

In the summer of 1989 Cargill began operation of its state-of-the-art beef packing plant in High River, Alberta. Cargill first announced that it would invest over $44-million in a beef slaughter, fabrication, rendering and hide operation at High River, Alberta, in October, 1987. At that time, Cargill's own publicity described the plant as "the only fully integrated, large beef facility in Canada . . . (with) full single-shift production of up to 6000 head per week."

Later reports gave the price tag at $53-million, with the Government of Alberta contributing at least $4-million in the form of a grant.

In the U.S., Cargill's Excel Corporation is the country's second or third largest beef packer. As Cargill describes it, "Excel specialises in slaughtering and cutting beef near its point of origin and shipping boxes of vacuum-packed cuts to markets in North America, Japan, and other export homes." (The three biggest beef packers in the U.S., ConAgra, IBP and Excel, between them produce 82% of U.S. boxed beef, the standard product that is shipped to retail outlets.[83]

The High River site was chosen, among other reasons, because 80% of the fat cattle produced in Canada are finished in Alberta and most of these come from within a 150 mile radius of High River.

A creative solution was found for dealing with the half-million gallons a day waste water that would be produced by the plant after Calgary sports fishermen objected to the dumping of the waste into the Bow River upstream of their favourite fishing holes. Eventually an agreement was reached with the Government of Alberta, the town of High River and Ducks Unlimited to pipe the waste water, after treatment, about ten miles south east to Frank Lake, which has been a dry lake bed in recent years. The shared costs of this part of the project were estimated at between $7.4 and $8.9-million.

Cargill, and the renovated Lakeside Packers (partly owned by Mitsubishi of Japan) in Brooks, Alberta, which between them can handle 45 percent of all the cattle available, intended to pay $9 per hour when they opened. At that time, the 700 workers at the four Canada Packers plants in Alberta would have their base wage rate of $12.51 averaged with wages at other local plants, including the new Cargill plant. This would mean a $1.50 per hour rollback in the basic wage of the Canada Packers workers. Canada Packers forced this concession from the workers in 1988 under threat of closing its plant altogether. Thus even a full year before its plant opened, Cargill, in effect, was able to set the basic wage rates for the packinghouse workers in the province of Alberta.

By October, 1989, union wages in the packing industry had dropped $1.25 an hour to a base wage of $11.25. Non-unionized Cargill Foods was at that time paying $9.00 an hour.[84]*

According to Cargill, its High River plant is the most efficient beef plant in North America, containing under one roof slaughter, processing, rendering, and production of green hides. The plant can produce boxed beef to the highest standards of quality and is able to supply specialized markets by contracting with nearby feedlot operators to produce to Cargill specifications.

Cargill is aiming for the high end of the market, with 25% going into eastern Canada and the rest eventually into Korea, Taiwan, and China. By late 1989 it had offices in Toronto, Montreal, and Moncton, N.B., to handle beef sales. Cargill also plans to take advantage of the Japanese market that it sees coming as a result of U.S. pressure on Japan to open its market to U.S. meat exports.

According to Cargill's Isman, the High River plant is to go a second shift early in 1990 and extend its cutting and packaging activities so that it can supply the country with cryovac (vacuum-packed and then frozen) retail cuts. The cryovac process extends the shelf-life of meat a minimum of 30 days from the cutting date. When the plant gets onto a double shift it should be able to supply about 10% of the total Canadian market for beef, according to Isman, while slaughtering about 15% of the national cattle slaughter. (Exports and imports account for the difference.)

Interestingly, while Cargill and the U.S. government are pressing the Korean government for permission for Cargill to

---

* In February, 1990, union workers at XL Beef in Calgary ended a lockout by accepting a weighted average rollback of $2.39. Threatening to replace them with non-union workers, the company had cited Cargill Foods' wage rates of $8 starting with a base rate of $9.60, and top hourly rate of $10.95.[85]

build a soybean processing facility in that country, the U.S. government is also pressing the Korean government to open up its market to "high quality U.S. beef cuts for use at hotels."[86] Could it be Cargill's Excel Corporation that is to be the supplier, or Cargill Foods of Canada?

> Cargill Foods, Brampton, Ontario, and the No Frills division of National Grocers Co. Ltd., [a division of Loblaws/Weston] is testing consumer response to case-ready fresh beef in the supermarket. The vacuum-packed beef cuts are sold under the brandname "Tender-cut". The beef is supplied by Excel, Cargill's U.S. beef packer, from its plant in Missouri. This is clearly a warm-up for the product of the High River plant.[87]

There are problems with this scenario, however. According to *Forbes* magazine:

> Excel Corp., part of Cargill Inc., produces a U.S. choice product that's sold in grocery stores in a vacuum pack that gives the meat a 35-day shelf-life. But the package also makes the meat look unusually dark and thus, to some, old and unappetizing. Despite years of effort and spending of "tens of millions of dollars," says Herb Meischen, Excel's marketing vice-president, consumption is dwindling and the product isn't profitable.[88]

There is more to Cargill in Alberta than their new High River plant. Cargill was already the major feed and feed supplement manufacturer and supplier before the packing plant was announced. Cargill also finances cattle through its Financial Services Division if a feedlot operator is short of cash. The stipulation is that the cattle that are financed by Cargill have to be raised on Nutrena feeds. In any case, the feeder has little choice, since no bank is apt to loan money for feed when the cattle are already assigned to Cargill as collateral for the loan with which they were purchased. If Cargill is then also the cattle buyer, it can tell the grower what specifications the cattle have to meet, when they will be shipped, and how much will be paid for them. The upshot is that the rancher or feedlot operator is, in effect, operating a franchise. At the same time, Cargill can put tremendous pressure on its "competition". In the fall and winter of 1989-90 it was widely reported that Cargill was paying top price for cattle in order to fill its plant capacity.

In addition to its low, non-union wages, which itself puts pressure on already existing plants, the bidding-up of cattle won't hurt a company with Cargill's resources in the short term, while it may drive its competitors out of business, particularly if Cargill is also undercutting the current wholesale price of beef. Art Child, President of Burns Foods of Calgary, was reported to have said that beef was being offered at 10-14 cents a pound below the market by Cargill, while normal profits are 3-4 cents per pound.[89] Buyers as far east as Nova Scotia reported that Cargill was "low-balling" the market in late 1989 in order to get established. This led some buyers to express their concern that this would wipe out any smaller packers who could not lose as much money as Cargill appeared prepared to do, in order to buy its way into the market.

In November, 1989, both Canadian Dressed Meats, a division of Burns Meats, and Canada Packers, the largest food manufacturer in Canada, announced the closing of their Ontario beef packing operations. The C.D.M. plant had a capacity of 2000 head per week and the Canada Packers Burlington plant a capacity of 4000 per week. This brought to seven the number of plants that closed down between September, 1988 and December, 1989, with a total capacity of 10,000 head per week. Most if not all of these plants were older and simply less efficient than Cargill's new High River plant, but whether they could have survived Cargill's assault on the marketplace is in doubt in any case. Some may have chosen to get out while they still had a choice.

From Cargill's standpoint, being the feed supplier, the banker, the buyer of the finished cattle, their butcher and their wholesaler, creates a tidy system that gives Cargill maximum control and return with the major risks – weather and animal health – being shouldered by others. It is also a very good way to market cheap grain, as long as you are not the farmer who grows it.

Cargill's hog operations in Canada exhibit the same policy. In Mount Lehman, British Columbia, Cargill operates a 27,000 hybrid hog breeding farm from which it supplies growers. In 1979 Cargill launched its Cargill Pork Systems in Manitoba. There a "qualified applicant" can enter into "a production agreement with C.P.S. under which he agrees to supply the land, buildings, equipment and production management."[90] "Production management" may be more commonly known as "labour".

Cargill, under such a contract, agrees "to provide the breeding stock, feed, veterinary assistance [advice], health aids [drugs] and ongoing technical and managerial support." Cargill has since then dropped its contract hog operations and is now simply the supplier of Nutrena Feeds and advice.

In mid-1989 the European Community banned the import of all beef raised with the help of synthetic hormones. The American and Canadian beef establishment let out a yelp of "unfair trade distortion" and the U.S. Government retaliated with tariffs on a list of EC exports. It wasn't long, however, before Cargill, through its subsidiary Excel, decided that it might be able to meet the European specifications for the 10,000 tonne "hormone-free" beef import quota. Interestingly, were Cargill to go ahead, this would effectively negate the U.S. government case that the hormone ban is simply a non-tariff trade restriction.[91]

Chapter 9

ONTARIO: A PLACE TO GROW

> The exponential increases in crop production, experienced around the world due to chemical and fertilizer-intensive agriculture, is just getting started ... In Canada, production will shift from the western provinces, where transportation remains an expensive proposition, to Ontario. This is where the action is, and that's why Cargill Grain has moved into the market.92

Prior to spring, 1988, Cargill was a minor presence in Ontario agriculture. With its acquisition of Maple Leaf Mills' 23 country elevators and mills and four grain terminals in early 1988, Cargill moved into the spotlight in Ontario. It added to its presence in early 1989 with the purchase of Cyanamid Canada's fertilizer operations, which consisted of 14 wholly-owned outlets plus six or so joint ventures. In June, 1989, it also purchased Arkona Feeds. By the end of 1989, Cargill had 31 locations for grain handling in Ontario, apart from the Thunder Bay terminals, and controlled about 21% of provincial storage capacity.93 (This increased concentration compares to the 11% control exercised by Maple Leaf Mills in 1983.) Rumours continue to circulate about additional acquisitions.

According to Cargill's Isman, Cargill moved into Ontario because Ontario has good grain production potential and good transportation, with ready access to water routes to both the U.S.

and the global market. Isman's predecessor, Ian Gillies, described to me how Cargill is now in a position to be "a more aggressive seller" of Ontario corn and soybeans, for "the benefit of the farmers, as well as to improve relations" with the Wheat Board of Ontario. Another reason may be that Ontario is a less regulated market. It is not part of the territory covered by the Canadian Wheat Board; and while there is the Ontario Wheat Marketing Board through which all Ontario wheat must be marketed, it is not as stringent or comprehensive as the Canadian Wheat Board and deals only with wheat.

Previously, as Gillies put it, Cargill did not have "originating capacity" for corn and soybeans, so if it made a sale it had to buy the grain or beans from another company. It also was not able to "control the variables". Besides, Ontario is "under-developed" in the use of "marketing tools" such as options, which are a way to increase sales and returns to farmers. This has been proved, he said, at Cargill's Talbotville, Ontario, elevator.[94]

It is widely recognized in the newly acquired Cargill feed facilities in Ontario that there is clear corporate policy to favour the feather (poultry) and hog accounts and discourage the small accounts, such as dairy or beef. Cargill wants the big bulk accounts, not the "nickel and dime" bagged accounts. Unless, that is, Cargill decides to challenge the co-ops with full-service facilities, which is what some local managers, both in and outside of Cargill, believe will be the case. This would be a minor step, since Cargill already has in its system seeds, chemicals, and fertilizers.

Cargill, in many communities, may soon be, if it is not already, the primary supplier of crop "inputs" – Cargill or Asgrow seed, Cargill fertilizer, Cargill chemicals – as well as the primary buyer of the crops harvested. In between Cargill is happy to supply soil tests and input recommendations while also advising on crop marketing, that is, on hedging, contracts, crop loans, and other financial services.

Cargill also supplies a "comment" to the farmers of Ontario in *Farm and Country*, a newspaper owned by the Ontario Federation of Agriculture, written by Pat Lynch, who is described as working "in agribusiness as a crop consultant." He is not identified as working for Cargill out of its Chatham, Ontario, office, but his article is consistent with the corporate line that one can read, in much more sophisticated form, in Cargill's *Bulletin* or hear in the speeches of Cargill executives. For example:

> Sustainable agriculture means different things to different people. One U.S. group [not identified] believes that sustainable agriculture is a system where producers buy next to no inputs. This Low Input Sustainable Agriculture (LISA) is practised by some who end up with low returns. For most farmers, LISA is little more than a talking point. JULIE will be their option. JULIE stands for Just Utilizing Least Inputs Efficiency. During the tough times of the 1980s farmers who followed JULIE survived. They soil tested . . . More than likely they also made wise and efficient use of pesticides, feed additives and antibiotics . . .[95]

Beans and Corn

In Alberta, as we saw, Cargill's interests are not limited to beef and barley. In the same way, selling seeds and fertilizer and trading in small grains is not all Cargill is doing in Ontario. Beans and corn are major Ontario cash crops and Cargill is keenly interested in both. Cargill could easily bid up the price of Ontario's corn and either turn it into feed in its Ontario mills (those it has acquired or has said it will build, as at Arkona) or send it to Ohio to its corn wet milling plant. (Cargill Inc. is a major producer of High Fructose Corn Syrup.) Cargill might lose money in the short term, but it would probably be left with a market less cluttered with competitors such as St. Lawrence Starch.

In fact, in November, 1989, St. Lawrence Starch announced the closing of its Ontario mill, saying it could not pay the Ontario price for corn and compete in the market with products made from corn purchased at the U.S. price. It claimed the price of Ontario corn was artificially high due to the import duty on U.S. corn coming into Ontario. St. Lawrence announced that it would continue to sell its products in Canada, but they would be imported from A. E. Staley, the second-largest corn wet miller in the United States, with whom St. Lawrence has had a working relationship for 40 years.[96] Staley is owned by the venerable sugar refiner Tate and Lyle of England, which in turn owns Redpath, Canada's largest sugar refiner. Given that High Fructose Corn

Syrup (HFCS) is generally considered a competitor to cane or beet sugar, it is worth noting that supposedly competing companies have the same common owner.

Soybeans, like corn, are a basic animal feed ingredient; or, like canola, they can be crushed to yield a high quality edible oil and a high-protein animal feed (soybean meal). Cargill is the biggest soybean processor in the U.S.A, with 30% of the market, and one of the biggest worldwide. ADM (Archer Daniels Midland) is Cargill's biggest competitor. Recently, Feruzzi Agricola Finanziaria SpA of Italy moved aggressively into the global soybean business. Feruzzi purchased Central Soya of the U.S. in 1987, making it the third largest processor of soybeans in the U.S. Central Soya owns Central Soya of Canada which in turn owns Victory Soya Mills of Toronto.

There are three large soybean mills in Ontario. Beside the Victory mill in Toronto, Central Soya bought the CVOP mill in Hamilton from Canada Packers in August, 1989. The third large mill, located in Windsor, is technically owned by United Cooperatives of Ontario, but is operated as a part of a joint ADM-UCO venture under the name Grainco. That leaves Cargill without its own processing facilities for soybeans, facing two competitors in the marketplace.

In this context it is not surprising that in May, 1989, Cargill initiated aggressive buying of soybeans and soybean futures (contracts for delivery at a specified future date) to cover both its own processing needs in the U.S. and its short-term contract obligations.

Terms of Trade

But that is not all. Cargill obviously has a major interest in soybean prices and availability as both processor and trader. After the fact, there seems to be little doubt that it was Cargill, along with ADM, who persuaded the Chicago Board of Trade to intervene in the futures market for soybeans and order Feruzzi to dispose of almost all of the soybean futures contracts it held in mid July: some 23-million bushels. To the regulators it could be made to appear that Feruzzi was trying to corner the market by purchasing contracts for virtually all the soybeans available. Feruzzi claimed that these beans were simply needed to supply its own mills so that it could meet its contractual obligations. Perhaps this was the case, or perhaps Feruzzi thought it could force some changes, for its benefit, in the somewhat cosy relationships between the traditional major players. What Feruzzi probably did not reckon on was the political muscle that Cargill and others can summon on their behalf.

> Feruzzi broke no rules in accumulating its position. But whatever the rationale behind it . . . the decision [of the CBOT] is a victory for America's Cargill in its battle to stay atop the world soybean trade. Indeed Cargill lobbied hard for the decision.[97]

The net effect of this whole business on the price of beans was to drive them down – which cannot but help benefit a trader and processor like Cargill. As the assistant chief commissioner of the Canadian Wheat Board said about Cargill Ltd. president Kerry Hawkins: "His bottom line depends on volume, not price."[98]

When the smoke cleared, it became apparent that both Cargill Inc., and some of its traders in their own names, were holding a lot of short contracts that they could not fill at the time of the CBOT intervention, so they had been purchasing beans at the November contract price plus a premium of more than $1.50. By mid-August, however, as a result of good weather coupled with the CBOT sell order to Feruzzi, November contract prices had dropped to US$5.64/bushel, the lowest price in 20 months. Under those conditions, it would not have been difficult for Cargill to buy beans cheap to fulfil its short contracts and make a good profit, having turned what could have been a disaster into a profit-making opportunity.

In its January, 1990, *Bulletin*, Cargill continued its explanation and defense of the futures market, and along the way the defense of its own actions in the case against Feruzzi:

> Stock declines and clandestine investigations gave way in the summer of 1989, however, to a more contentious issue: the Chicago Board of Trade's emergency action in connection with July soybean futures contracts . . .

> The July 10 order brought this to a head . . . *Some market participants* had indicated broader concern that some futures contracts were no longer reflecting the cash markets that underlie them, thus adversely affecting their ability to serve as legitimate means of hedging and transferring price risk.

> These twin complaints left the CBOT and the CFTC [Chicago Futures Trading Commission] in increasingly difficult positions. Both had been accused of being uninvolved and passive in the probe of pit-trading abuses but ironically now were criticized for their aggressiveness in trying to protect the market. *(emphasis added)*

Beyond the issue of trading, however, are even greater stakes for companies like Cargill, ADM and Feruzzi.

> World demand for both vegetable oil and protein meal has been growing at an annual rate of about 4% in recent years. Yet, U.S. sunflower and soybean production has declined by about one-fifth since 1979. South American farmers have increased their soybean area by the same 12.5 million acres lost in the U.S. Soybeans account for roughly half the tonnage of all oilseeds produced worldwide.[99]

Feruzzi, Bunge and Born, and Archer Daniels Midland all have significant oilseed producing areas they can draw on outside of the U.S. where Cargill is strongest. It is perfectly logical, then, that Cargill should want to increase its control over the U.S. supply and gain a significant measure of control in the Canadian soybean market. This objective also adds weight to Cargill's campaign for a "free market" in North American grains.

The Seed Business

We have taken a look at some of Cargill's activities relating to corn and soybeans. Canola (low eurucic acid rapeseed) is the third of the important high-value oilseeds, and the range of products that can be produced from canola is much greater than that which can be produced from corn due to the relative ease with which canola can be genetically manipulated. Cargill is now the #2 supplier of canola seed in North America as a result of its purchase, in the summer of 1989, of the assets of Canola, Inc., which markets canola seed in the states of Ohio, Michigan, Illinois, Indiana, and Kentucky. Cargill already marketed Canola Inc. seed through its own distribution system.

This acquisition seems to typify Cargill development policy. If there is an area in which the company is weak, rather than building from scratch it seems to prefer to buy an existing business that is in the area into which it wishes to expand. Thus it paid far more for the Ontario grain operations of Maple Leaf Mills than anyone else thought they were worth, but then Cargill got where it wanted to go in a hurry.

Unlike fertilizer, or even chemicals, seeds are constantly changing in their characteristics, demands, and applications. To be a player in the seed business requires research. Like other corporations, Cargill has responded to the urging of the Conservative government to invest in university research with the assurance that it will be able to reap the benefits of work carried out in publicly supported institutions. In 1985 Cargill established a five-year, $375,000 fund to aid plant and animal research at Canadian universities and research stations.

> The first grant made from the new Cargill fund was $45,000 to support a student . . . in the area of protoplast fusion. This procedure could combine in one canola plant both triazine tolerance and male sterility – a characteristic required for economic production of hybrid seed.[100]

Concentration on hybrids has been part of Cargill strategy throughout the past decade. By 1981 Cargill's wheat breeding program in Argentina was devoted 100% to hybrid work. Cargill began its work in France in earnest in 1966 with corn, its first northern Europe hybrid being registered in 1971; by 1981 the program in France was nearly 80% in hybrids. Cargill has developed hybrids in canola, sunflower, and corn for France, Germany and Spain.[101]

There are some intimate relationships in agribusiness at the level of the seed. For example: in May, 1988, it was reported that corn growers in southwestern Ontario were getting 35 cents per bushel premium on waxy hybrid corn from Cargill. Wondering at this apparent generosity, I discovered that Cargill is under contract to supply corn to National Starch of Canada. (Along the way I discovered that National Starch is owned by Unilever, another giant transnational food company.) All NaCan crops are based on American hybrids imported under an agreement with Agriculture Canada that ensures that all seed from the hybrids goes to NaCan.[102] So Cargill was bound to fulfill its contract and its apparent generosity to the corn producers was, in fact, necessity and self-interest.

Seed sales are, of course, a logical extension for any "crop input" supplier. One-stop shopping has considerable appeal for a farmer at seeding time. Attractive financing can be arranged if the same company who will buy the crop is also the supplier of seed, fertilizer and chemicals ("crop protection agents" as they are now referred to); and chances are the same outfit will provide soil analysis and crop input recommendations. If the seed supplied is hybrid, the farmer must return to the source year after year for fresh seed, rather than engaging in the traditional practice of saving the best grain from the crop to be planted next year as seed. It is easy to see how a farmer could quickly become dependent on such convenience and accessible expertise. On the other hand, such a system would be diametrically opposed to organic or ecological agriculture. Sustainable systems require much more localization of knowledge as well as decision-making, to say nothing of the aim of ecological agriculture to reduce off-farm inputs and dependency.

THE CARGILL CROP INPUTS PRODUCTION PROGRAM

Reprinted from a handout for Saskatchewan farmers

This is a traditional time to take advantage of low prices offered for tax buying purposes. However, with tight cash flows we do not expect an abundance of interest and activity.

We have a program to ease your mind and cash flow for 1990. We are offering Crop Input Production Contracts for wheat, barley, canola, canary seed, flax and mustard.

Contract Outline

1. With an approved credit agreement we determine a maximum credit line calculated on a crop acre basis. We allow $30.00 of inputs per acre for all crops contracted. . .

You would be able to purchase a maximum of . . . inputs and place it on a "non interest" bearing account payable on Oct. 17, 1990.

2. You are charged a surcharge of 3.5% on the "competitive" selling price for fertilizer and pesticides. . .

3. A Crop Insurance Indemnity form is signed if you carry crop insurance.

4. If you don't carry crop insurance or your credit line is more than $15,000 we ask that you sign a Security Agreement with us.

5. Purchases of inputs must be made the spring of 1990.

Grain Obligations

1. The grain produced on the contracted acres must be delivered to Cargill.

2. The grain must be delivered before July 31, 1991.

3. The grain doesn't have to be priced out for the contract. It can be priced at any time before delivery or delivered on a Price Basis Contract and priced out before the 90th day or sold and exchanged for futures, in the case of non-boards.

4. You do not have to specify a specific grade or amount of tonnes on these contracts. Whatever grade or amount you grow we will purchase.

continued next page

Payment of Accounts

Your account can be paid any time before Oct. 17th with either a cheque or grain delivery. If your account is not paid on Oct. 17th the account goes into our regular interest bearing account at a cost of 1.75% per month. . . .

Is It A Good Deal

Yes, definitely . . . calculates out to an annual interest rate of approximately 7-9% . . .

Are We Competitive

Yes!

1. If barley is good enough for malt, we will buy it.

2. Our grain prices are "super" competitive and we periodically offer spot premiums to enhance deliveries. . . .

Deadline For Signup

This offer is good until next spring, however . . . we urge you to come in and start the process before Jan. 31, 1990.

Thank you.

Cargill Ltd.
Speers, Sask.

Chapter 10

PERSONNEL AND POLITICS

"We have a business plan to become something more than a country-based Western grain company." – Kerry Hawkins, President of Cargill, Ltd.[103]

Cargill is known for running a tight ship and demanding loyalty of its employees. They tend to be young and aggressive, and can look forward to a long future with the company if they serve it well. Barbara Isman described the company to me as "just a bunch of people trying to make a living – a family company." She also added, with tongue in cheek, presumably, that "We are badly organized – policy is really not all that well worked out."

It is an interesting approach to the notion of a family. The assistant manager of one of the Ontario Cyanamid facilities that Cargill bought in 1989 said that Cargill never spoke to him at the time and never asked if he wanted to work for Cargill. Cargill never even told the staff that they had bought the business. At other facilities that Cargill has purchased, employees say that nothing has changed except the name on the invoices, and that Cargill has never talked with them about policies, plans, or prices. I talked with local Cargill managers at many locations in the U.S. and Canada and their comments were virtually identical. "We didn't know anything about it until it happened" was the way the manager of one of the Maple Leaf Mills facilities described the Cargill take-over.

Local managers – from Dixon, California, to Ayr, Ontario– all say that they are running "free standing" businesses. A feed mill manager says he buys and sells grain wherever he can get the best price, with no preference for other Cargill companies. Nor are Cargill buyers given preferred status. *If* this is actually the case, it makes practical business sense in a corporation the size of Cargill. However, hearing the identical sentences from local managers in every type of facility in different provinces makes it begin to sound more like ideology than practice, or as a non-Cargill executive put it, like they all read it off the same set of orders. Of course this also begs the rather crucial question of where the money goes and where policy *is* set.

Visiting Cargill facilities across the country is an interesting way to organize an itinerary. Asking questions across the country about a company like Cargill is also a good way to find out what a company is like in human terms.

One ex-employee told me that while Cargill was a good company to learn from and had a highly developed screening process for new employees, they still lost a lot of employees after five or six years who went to work for other companies that paid better and provided better working conditions. As another ex-Cargill employee put it, his boss in Cargill wanted to know what he was doing, when he did it, why he did it, what else he was going to do and why he was going to do it. Other ex-employees of Cargill told me that they enjoyed their work and felt that both they and the company were doing a good job.

I have also been told that up to two years ago Cargill had a policy of hiring senior management from within the company and of not taking back any employee who left. Now that policy has changed and they are hiring outsiders as well as taking back previous employees.

Of course, some of those previous employees were really away for awhile on company business, as it were, acting as policy advisors to governments. Business executives are not likely to be found in elected positions in the Canadian Government – we seem to have a great preference for lawyers – but that matters little if they are welcome to act as senior policy advisors or work for Agriculture Canada under the federal Executive Exchange Program.

David Gilmore is a good example of Cargill's policy of shifting senior management through key public policy positions. Gilmore, at the time a Cargill vice-president, moved to Agriculture Canada in 1985, just after the Tory election victory, under the Executive Exchange Program. There he became coordinator of commodity strategy development. In 1987 he rejoined Cargill and went to the United States to learn the meat trade. When he returned to Canada, Gilmore became manager of eastern Canadian meat sales for Cargill Foods. (Cargill Foods is the operating arm of Cargill responsible for the High River packing plant and the sale of its products.)

Phil de Kemp is another example of how people move between the corporate sector, Agriculture Canada, and the government. Such movement can be justified, of course, in that the country benefits by the accumulated expertise of people who have been trained to know the whole system, in this case, grains and oilseeds. But this assumes that knowledge is neutral and that there is no divergence of interest between, say, farmers, corporations, and the people as a whole as represented by the government. The question remains, whose interests and whose policies do these people serve?

De Kemp told me that he went to work for Cargill in the commodities marketing division in 1983 when he finished university. He worked in three locations getting to know Cargill and western grains and oilseeds. Then in 1986, as a Cargill employee, he went to work with Agriculture Canada under the Executive Exchange Program, during which time Cargill continued to pay him. When that term expired in September, 1988, he stayed on, becoming an employee of Agriculture Canada. A year later he was "loaned" to Charlie Mayer, MP, Minister for Grains and Oilseeds, as special assistant for western grains and oilseeds. He was able to move about this freely because the rules of the civil service, which prohibit a civil servant from working for private industry or government in the field of his expertise for two years after leaving the civil service, did not apply since technically he was never a civil servant, in spite of the work he was doing.

De Kemp, while no longer a Cargill employee, has a valuable history to bring to Tory policy formation. Under the Executive Exchange Program he actually started working with the Grain Marketing Bureau when it was in the Department of External Affairs. Mayer had the Bureau moved to his jurisdiction in Agriculture Canada, and de Kemp went with it. The subsequent move from the Grain Marketing Bureau to Mayer's office would have been little more than a formality. When I asked who was paying his salary, de Kemp would say only that he is paid by the Government of Canada.[104]

One of the results of this process is well illustrated by a memo signed by the Deputy Minister of Agriculture, Jean Jacques Noreau:

> The principles for agriculture policy reform presented in Cargill's brief are consistent with government policy direction.[105]

Another Canadian example is Barbara Isman, Director of Corporate Relations (foreign affairs, or public relations) for Cargill in Winnipeg, who, as already noted in the discussion of the Canadian Wheat Board, was Executive Director of the Western Canadian Wheat Growers Association at the time it was created out of Palliser Wheat Growers Association in 1985. Isman remained in that position until she resigned abruptly at the end of 1987. In December, 1985, the new WCWGA launched a glossy magazine with Barbara Isman as Senior Editor. The name of the magazine is *Pro-Farm*. In her first editorial, Isman explained that the name stood for "progressive" and "professional". In that same issue there was an ad with a bold heading which read, "A Partnership That Works" in which "Cargill Ltd. congratulates *Pro-Farm* on its first issue". As a staff member of the WCWGA Isman was a member of the SAGIT – Sectoral Advisory Group for International Trade. (SAGITs were the most-favoured advisory groups for the Canada-U.S. trade deal.) And of course Western Canadian Grain Growers is one of the growing number of right-wing commodity lobby groups that effectively represent corporate interests, like those of the grain or agri-chemical companies.

Let this not be misunderstood as a personal attack. Naming specific people, as I have done, does not imply that they are evil or that I hold them personally responsible for corporate policy.

What I have described here has been aptly labelled *"structural corruption"*.[106]

Real people do, nevertheless, make real policy decisions, and real people implement them. Naming the individuals involved is one way of clarifying a situation which is often mystified by the use of the passive or future tense, with no subject of the verb or sentence – as if events simply *happen*.

In the U.S., Cargill executives move in similar patterns. Daniel Amstutz, a twenty-five year Cargill veteran, was U.S. Undersecretary for International Affairs and Commodity Programs 1983-87. Since then he has been a leader of the U.S. trade commission in the GATT negotiations on agricultural trade.

One well-informed source also reported that at the December 1988 GATT meeting in Montreal, two of the U.S. negotiators were Cargill employees.

Cargill is certainly not the only company to behave this way, and Canada is hardly the only country to experience a symbiotic relationship between the government and certain corporate interests. In fact, one might wonder if the model that Cargill Ltd. is pursuing in Canada is not that of Argentina. There, when a heart attack killed Economy Minister Roig in the new Menem government within days of Menem taking office, Menem turned to the Argentine president of Brazilian-based Bunge and Born (sales of $15 billion) for suggestions of a replacement. It was a logical step, since Roig himself had been a Bunge and Born executive. The result was the appointment of Nestor Rapanelli to the position of Economy Minister. Rapanelli was, prior to this appointment, head of Bunge and Born in Argentina. Argentina is, of course, a major grains producer and exporter, and it is now Rapanelli's job "to carry out the Bunge and Born plan, a strategy for shifting Argentina from disastrous state intervention and protectionism to a market-driven economy."[107]

Respected farm writer Barry Wilson, after a recent visit to Argentina, reported that President Menem,

> has announced a series of privatization moves designed to reduce the size and cost of government. Included among these is sale or lease of the terminal grain elevators owned by the National Grain Board and a reduction in grain board powers to influence domestic wheat prices

> ... Many farmers ... are fighting a reduction in the powers of the National Grain Board because they believe it will lower grain prices to farmers and will give the large grain companies more power.[108]

This is a good example of the problem that a Canadian farmer, or anyone else might have, in trying to understand the forces at work shaping the world in which they are trying to function. Either Wilson was unaware of the relationship between the government of Menem and the grain company Bunge and Born, or he did not realize its significance. The parallel in the relationships and policy objectives between Bunge and Born and the Argentine government and Cargill and the Canadian government should certainly have been pointed out one way or another. In neither case is there a need for a conspiracy theory. Lower prices for grain and more power for themselves are corporate objectives – and farmers have good reason to be concerned.

A careful screening of senior trade and agricultural policy officials both in Canada and many other countries would probably yield a good many similar illustrations of Cargill's unwillingness to leave its fortunes to chance or public will.

> Although Cargill loudly proclaims the need for free trade and abhors government regulation, it would be impossible for it to operate without the continued support of many state institutions and organizations.

> Wm. Pearce, [senior vice-president of Cargill Inc.] was a leading architect of the Williams Commission Report which drew up the blueprint of US agriculture in the 1970s. [He was then a *former* Cargill vice-president.][109]

Another indicator of the close association between certain corporate interests and their government agents is reflected in the figures of corporate, and corporate personnel, contributions to political parties. *(see table).* Cargill and its senior executives Kerry Hawkins and Richard Dawson (referred to as "Robert Dawson" and "R. Dawson" in the Elections Canada information from which these figures were obtained) have been consistent contributors to the Conservative Party. They have given much smaller amounts to the Liberal Party. It is perhaps only coincidental, or it may be company policy, but in the soybean upheaval in the summer of 1989 there was the same pattern: both the corporation itself and individual corporate executives were involved.

Of the Canadian grain companies, Richardson (Pioneer Grain) has been the other notable contributor to the Conservative Party. (The most striking figures in the list of political contributions by agribusiness are the contributions to the Tories by Nabisco: $51,825 in 1987 and $102,983 in 1988!)

For those not familiar with recent Canadian history, it should only be necessary to point out that Brian Mulroney and his Conservative Party were first elected in 1984 and then re-elected in 1988. The 1988 election focused on the Tory program of deregulation, privatization, "free trade" and general servitude to corporate interests.

In addition to the direct contributions to political parties, there are other ways to express political support. The Canadian Alliance for Trade and Job Opportunities raised and spent more than $5-million in the pro-free trade campaign of the Tories before the 1988 election. Cargill was among the companies refusing to reveal its contributions to this campaign.[110]

Contributions by Agribusiness

	1988 P.C.	1987 Lib.	1987 P.C.	1986 Lib.	1986 P.C.	1985 Lib.	1985 P.C.	1984 Lib.	1984 P.C.	Lib.
Cargill	$15,000	3,924	20,225	5,000	10,892	3,180	10,000	3,204	15,454	15,132
Kerry Hawkins	1,000		1,000		1,000		1,000		1,000	102
R. Dawson	1,000				550				1,150	
James Richardson	45,000	4,000	15,000							

source: Elections Canada

SECTION V: MOVIN' IT

Chapter 11

TRANSPORTATION

~~~~~~

Cargill's success is due in no small part to its innovation. Its operational philosophy is clearly stated in the words of Robbin Johnson, Cargill Inc. vice-president, public affairs:

> The development of modern transportation, storage and handling systems has made it possible to move huge quantities of foodstuffs great distances. This can be done economically, in a timely manner and in the desired qualities and conditions various buyers seek . . . Technologically, in other words, it has become possible to depend upon distant food supplies to meet a growing proportion of both basic needs and dietary improvements. A more diverse diet, more attractively priced, is now readily available. The principal impediments to achieving food security through imports now involve trade policies.[111]

> Transportation figures prominently in Cargill's manipulation of the domestic market. Since World War II, the development of new transportation techniques has enabled the company to stay one step ahead of its competitors and to extract the maximum profit from every bushel of grain it handles. In the late 1940s it opened a new route via the Minnesota River south of Minneapolis. Much of the technology and efficiency that characterizes the low-cost vegetable and oil industry was developed by Cargill. So were transportation and distribution innovations, such as the export of oil and meal in bulk . . .

In large measure, Cargill's growth is related to its progress in transportation.[112]

Oil and meal are not the only bulk cargoes Cargill has learned to handle. A company trade brochure titled *Cargill World of Juices* (c. 1987) tells of their innovation in orange juice marketing:

> Cargill pioneered the change from drum shipment to bulk storage and transportation. The result was consistently higher quality at a savings, thanks to a more uniform product, reduced labour, less product loss during handling, and faster delivery.

> Today Cargill owns and operates two bulk vessels, in addition to bulk storage and distribution terminals at our plants in Bebedourno and Uchoa, Brazil and in the ports of Santos, Brazil, Amsterdam, and Port Elizabeth, New Jersey.

In 1982 Cargill opened the largest floating feed products transfer facility in the world at Mile 158 in the Mississippi River. The export terminal, run by Cargill subsidiary Rogers Terminal and Shipping Co., was designed to transfer oilseed meals, corn gluten feed pellets, rice bran pellets and cottonseed meal from barges to ocean-going vessels more efficiently than land-based elevators.[113]

An interesting illustration of Cargill's underlying philosophy can be see in its activities in the port city of Stockton, California. The Port of Stockton is actually 75 miles inland, by deep water channel, from the San Francisco Bay bridge. Being that far inland puts it in the middle of the agricultural valley of California. There Cargill has, or is developing, six different facilities:

- the Nutrena feed mill mentioned earlier;
- a new flour mill (announced in May, 1989, this $16-million mill will be Cargill's 15th in the U.S.) to be located close to the Nutrena mill at the south end of the city;
- a feed supplement plant located in the port that utilizes molasses from Hawaii to produce Mol Mix liquid feed supplement;
- a new food-grade corn syrup distribution terminal to receive corn syrup in bulk in Cargill's own rail cars and distribute high fructose corn syrups, sweetener blends and corn-derived products to food processors of all kinds in both Canada and the U.S.;

- a recently-purchased fertilizer plant (Co-pal Fertilizer);
- the port facility itself for import and export of grains (while safflower goes entirely to Japan, wheat can go almost anywhere: I saw a Greek ship being loaded for the Soviet Union).

In trying to understand the context of Cargill's Canadian operations, it should also be noted that Cargill has a terminal in Pasco, Washington, from which it can ship grain by barge down the Columbia River to Portland, Oregon, for transfer to ocean-going ships. Barge traffic also moves on the Snake River from Pasco all the way to Lewiston, Idaho.

The Canadian Grain Transportation System

In recent years there has been a relentless attack, in the name of efficiency and modernization, on Canada's historic grain transportation system and policy. It is important, then, to remember that, as we noted in Chapter 2 on the Canadian Grain Marketing System, that it was the experience of drought and depression in the 1920s, combined with their experience of the rapaciousness of the bankers and grain traders, which caused the farmers of the Canadian Prairies to take a strong hand in defending their own interests. They formed the Prairie Wheat Pools and other cooperatives and forced the government to legislate into existence the Canadian Wheat Board. All of these institutions were established on the principle that every farmer should be treated fairly and with equity, and without discrimination because of where their homestead was located. Grain elevators and villages were established every seven to ten miles along the railways to serve the small mixed farms that produced the wheat for export so that no farmer had to travel with his or her grain more than a horse (or oxen) could travel in a day – to and from. (The steam locomotives had to be watered equally often.) In 1935 there were 5728 elevators on the prairies.

The Wheat Board was the farmers' guarantee that all farmers would receive the same price for their grain, regardless of where they lived or when they delivered the grain. On this basis the Wheat Board was able to contract for sales, knowing that it could call for the grain when it was needed.

Needless to say, the bankers, merchants and traders and railway companies involved in some aspect of the grain sector never have cared much for this system since its purpose has always been to eliminate speculation and undue profit. The principle of the Pools and the CWB was to pay fairly for grain and for services rendered, and not for anything else. Ever since the beginning the traders have been trying to break the system – even though those captains of industry who have relied on a large industrial labour force may well have been thankful that there has always been a good supply of cheap food to satisfy their often underpaid workers.

Cargill, for example, "invented" the *unit train* in the United States, according to its own publicity. The unit train is a string of specially designed hopper cars with which Prairie farmers are familiar in conjunction with the policy of what is called *variable rates*. These are discount rates offered at specific elevators and terminals for loading a large number of grain cars as one unit. WCWGA boasts that it was the organizer of the first unit train in Canada in 1973.

Unit trains served the purposes of large corporate grain shippers and large inland grain terminals; as Gilmore expressed it, "the unit train was an example of modernization that created both efficiencies and gross inequities."[114]

Producer cars, on the other hand, are primarily attractive to the larger farmers who harvest enough grain – often non-Board specialty crops like canola and flax – at one time to fill a whole hopper railcar. Producer cars are ordered by a producer (i.e. farmer) for a specific location. The producer will then fill the car directly from a truck with grain either right off the field or out of his own storage. The rail siding, which the producer car utilizes, has a symbiotic relationship to the elevator: without the elevator there would be no siding. The large producer – the only one who can fill a car – is given a preferred rate by the railroad, at the expense of the smaller producer. Up to the end of 1989 the farmer who utilized producer cars was still required to pay his or her share of the elevator costs, but aggressive farmers, and their commodity associations like the Western Barley Growers or the Western Canadian Wheat Growers Association, lobbied for and got a reduction in this charge. They would like to do away with it altogether, naturally, and free themselves to be even more "competitive" at the expense of others. Some smaller grain companies welcomed such a move that undercut the Prairie Pools and their smaller elevators.

The large companies, on the other hand, cannot count simply on producer cars; they require a larger volume that only the Pools and the Wheat Board can deliver (at this time). However, Cargill can gain considerable leverage if it can deal directly with a few large farmers who think they are being smart businessmen by taking advantage of the publicly supported infrastructure to get a better price in the short run.

The long and heated debate over the abandonment of smaller branch lines of the railroad and the building of very large inland terminals to replace local elevators are earlier (1970s-1980s) expressions of the same objectives being pursued by the private grain traders and their "free market" allies in government, universities and agriculture.

The elimination of the Crows Nest Pass freight rate, the introduction of variable rates – actually discounts for location and volume – unit trains and producer cars are all steps to eliminate fairness and equity and to make room for speculators and the purported advantages of "economies of scale." In the name of the free market, as Richard Gilmore pointed out in 1982,

> current deregulation reforms and volume-related fee structures geared toward competition in the transportation sector may thus result in a paradoxical situation of increased concentration.[115]

He is right except about the results being paradoxical: concentration *is* the aim. The rhetoric about competition is only for the farmers and the public.

It is not only the smaller farms that are the victims of this centralizing drive. Many rural communities, whose very existence as rural service centres was based on the local elevator, have had their economic base pulled out from under them and gradually the towns themselves wither and die. *Bigger is better is more efficient* makes bad social policy. In addition, this social policy has seldom been publicly debated, in spite of much heated debate about the issue of branch line abandonment and changes in the Crow Rate. The decisions are usually made in corporate boardrooms in Toronto or Minneapolis, or in the offices of the federal government in Ottawa.

In the U.S., agricultural policy has always been the subject of public discussion and congressional debate leading to specific agricultural policy legislation, however flawed the process may be in practice. In Canada, however, farm policy is created by a consultative process between industry and government, and set by committee and Cabinet – a form of "gentlemen's agreement" – without legislation and the public debate normally associated with policy legislation (as noted in the discussion of grains policy in Chapter 2). The Mulroney regime has carried this to a new extreme with its attitude that public and legislative debate is a nuisance, a brake on progress and an insult to "efficiency".

I said at the beginning that Cargill plays its game very well, and we need to keep this in mind. But Cargill's is only one among many possible games, and only one among the historic alternatives. If innovation, technology, and efficiency are all considered socially and morally neutral, then Cargill should be cheered on without restraint. But in the context of the longer term, of the broader interests of the human community and of what is ecologically sustainable, Cargill's brand of innovation may leave a great deal to be desired.

The president of Cargill's U.S. flour milling division summed up Cargill's attitude toward innovation:

> The future can successfully be met if we plan for it and if we are prepared to spend money to position ourselves for it . . . When you really start changing the way people think about things and the way they approach things is when you really start to get results.[116]

Chapter 12

TRANSPORTATION POLICY

~~~~~~

> In Canada, Cargill is expanding feed operations, and promoting con-
> tract production [of oilseeds and barley – non-CWB crops] . . . Their
> contract plan features floor prices with an open ceiling, indicating a
> greater interest in the control of commodities than commodity prices
> *per se* . . . Cargill . . . is strategically locating its terminals to facilitate
> southern shipment . . . Other Cargill strategy calls for the support of
> abolition of the Crow's Nest Pass rates in order to make their rates
> at the Gulf of Mexico more competitive . . .[117]

At the beginning of 1990, Cargill and ADM started offering
minimum price contracts in Ontario.[118] For the farmer, these are
little different than the Canadian Wheat Board's initial price. In
other words, the private traders are trying to match the accepted
practices of the CWB in the hopes of fooling the farmers.

Milt Fair, the chief executive officer of the Saskatchewan
Wheat Pool, told guests at a banquet celebrating the opening of a
new Pool elevator in Weyburn, Saskatchewan, that foreign grain
companies stand to benefit from a change in Canada's grain marketing and transportation system. "There are representatives of
organizations from outside our country who are working very dili-
gently to see a change in our system," he said. "I think it is time

producers started to realize a good deal of the pressure is coming from organizations not based in this country." [119]

Until very recently Cargill's role in Canadian agriculture appeared to be quite limited. It operated primarily in the Prairie grain areas – the same territory covered by the Canadian Wheat Board – and was simply one grain agent among several operating in the rather narrow space assigned to such companies outside the domain of the CWB. But as indicated earlier, it has consistently sought to undermine the authority and jurisdiction of the Wheat Board, usually on grounds of efficiency or rationalization or some other such ideological argument. It has done this by working, in its own ways, for the erosion of CWB power and for the destruction of the national grain transportation policy (Crows Nest Pass Freight Rate, the At-and-East Rate, Feed Freight Assistance) that was established decades ago. But if Cargill has been the leader, it certainly has not been alone. Pioneer Grain (James Richardson and Sons), Continental, Parrish & Heimbecker and others would have been rooting for the same team.

The Crow's Nest Pass statutory freight rates go back to 1897. From 1924 to 1983 the rates for rail transport of grains and oilseeds were regulated by the federal government. With the passage of Bill C-155 in 1983 the statutory Crow rates were abolished but grain transport remained regulated under the Western Grain Transportation Act. The Crow "benefit", roughly $700-million per year, became payable directly to the railroads. Thus the railroads could keep the rates charged farmers "artificially" low while collecting a subsidy from the federal government.

This policy has kept Prairie grain production essentially oriented to the export market – the only market, in fact, given the volume of grain – since the full costs of grain transportation have not been paid by the exporters (which are grain companies and not farmers) but by the public in the form of government subsidy to the railroads. The Prairie Pools, the National Farmers Union, and the CWB have continued to press for retention of this form of payment to the railroads, while the private traders and their "rent seeking" commodity group supporters have lobbied frantically for the benefit to be paid to the farmers. If this shift is made, it will free the railroads to charge whatever they wish, and to rationalize their lines as they choose. The effect will be a major achievement in the Conservative campaign towards complete deregulation. Lest this be interpreted simply as a goal of the Conservative Party, it must be pointed out that the Liberals, in the person of Otto Lang, among others, have long shared the same objective.

Railways: Capturing Subsidies

In September, 1989, it was reported that the federal government was ready to consider paying the $700-million subsidy to individual farmers rather than to the railroads, if it could be shown that paying it to the railroads is inhibiting diversification of the Prairie economy.[120] What appears to be meant by diversification is the expansion of the Alberta cattle feed-lot industry (since the subsidy would no longer be tied to grain exports) and the further-processing of grains on the Prairies. (Sask. Pool likes to refer to its donut chain – Robin's – as this sort of diversification.) The implication of this, given the scale being discussed, is either that Canada would become a massive exporter of noodles, bread and cookies, or that Canadians would increase their consumption of these "breadstuffs" 1000 or 1-million-fold! Proponents of the pay-the-producer faction claim, however, that it would lead to diversification into both livestock and what are referred to as specialty crops, i.e., non-CWB grains and oilseeds. There is *no* indication that the diversification referred to is in the direction of sustainable agriculture and a real diversification and balance of crops.

The effect of pay-the-producer, for Cargill, would be the best of both worlds: lower feed grain prices and hence lower priced cattle and continuing low prices for grain for export, both the result of public subsidies paid to the farmer but benefitting the feeders, processors and exporters.

Were the subsidy to be paid directly to the farmers, they could, in theory, choose either to feed the grain to livestock or to export it. Given that Cargill has become the major Canadian meat packer, while at the same time increasing its presence as a grain exporter, it would serve Cargill's interests to have a choice between subsidized grain or subsidized cattle. Cargill would likely pay less for finished cattle, knowing that the grain cost was lowered by the amount of the subsidy. As with most subsidies, it would be the processor or exporter that ends up with the benefit, not the primary producer, in this case the cattle feeder. (It is perhaps necessary at this point to note that increasing overall livestock production and, with it, meat consumption is *not* a real alternative, nor is a large increase in exports.)

Towards the end of 1989 the attacks on the grain handling system steadily increased. Western Canadian Wheat Growers, United Grain Growers, the railroads, the trucking companies, and a host of other vested interests joined the clamour to change the method of payment of the Crow benefit and "rationalize" the grain handling system. As Cargill vice-president Dick Dawson has said, $300-million or about $10 per export tonne of grain could be saved by abandoning low-volume branch lines. However, as pointed out by the Alberta Pool:

> A branchline abandonment is more a cost transfer from the railways and the federal government to farmers than it is a net saving. Farmers have to buy larger trucks and incur more trucking expenses when a branchline is closed. It is misleading to equate savings secured by the railway as a net saving to the grain production, handling and transportation industry.[121]

Cargill has, however, been arguing for abandonment of branch lines for many years. In 1976 Cargill drew up a list of 858 miles of branch lines which it felt could be abandoned. Cargill at that time also argued that the Crow benefits be paid directly to the farmers and that producers be given the right to load their own platform cars.[122]

The kind of attitude that is being fostered in this attack on a system organized on the principle of equality is well expressed in an article in a special section of UGG's *Grainews* "sponsored by CN" (Canadian National railway):

> It must be argued that it is not the fault of a farmer living near a more efficient rail line that another farmer chose to reside in a remote area served by a little-used branch line. The former has no moral obligation to subsidize the latter, owing to the fact that a civilized society must recognize each individual's right to freedom of choice and freedom of action.[123]

In its *Presentation to Finance Canada*,[124] Cargill set out its current policy recommendations on grain transportation. Pointing out that "farmers themselves have changed" and that "greater degrees of management skills, diverse debt levels, greater variation in farm size and production choice can be seen on prairie farms", the Cargill paper concludes that "It is time to move away from the traditional 'farming' mentality towards a well-considered modernized and integrated agriculture framework." Among the policy reforms that Cargill calls for, transportation policy is at the head of the list:

> The structure of railway compensation is production and trade distorting, prohibits economically efficient movement of grain, and has reduced infrastructure investment.

Cargill therefore calls for replacing the current form of Western Grain Transportation Act subsidy – the "Crow benefit" – with a "neutral payment mechanism"; "the elimination of distance-based rail rates in favour of cost-related rate pricing"; and a fixed schedule for branchline abandonment and rehabilitation.

To understand these recommendations, however, one must also understand Cargill's basic objectives, which they also set forth in this policy paper.

• visibility of market signals to farmers
• aggressive pursuit of market opportunities
• economically efficient and environmentally sustainable allocation of resources
• conformity to international trade laws
• an economic environment which allows the long-term maintenance of healthy infrastructures.

All this sounds fine by itself, but what it translates into, in their words, is:

• trade liberalization
• multilateral agreement on agricultural trade, including elimination of "trade distorting subsidies and practices"
• income support mechanism that is "predictable, individually responsive, market and trade neutral" and voluntary.
• "reduce marketing controls on domestic buyers to allow competitive sourcing of raw products"
• elimination of quota restrictions on non-CWB grains.

Cargill terminal, Thunder Bay

Cargill Port, Minneapolis

The benefit that Cargill sees resulting from its policy recommendations is "enhanced economic viability" for "the agriculture industry", with possibilities such as "expanded livestock production, increased crop production choice and value-added opportunities." Their policy paper, however, does not give any indication of what these opportunities might actually be or who will benefit from them if they actually do exist. It is clear, however, that what Cargill is after is the lowest possible price for its raw materials, whether that is wheat for export, cattle for slaughter, canola for crushing, or soybeans for feed.

The real issue, according to Cargill's Dawson, is the trade-off between the survival of the basic Western Canadian family farm as we know it and retaining a vital export competitiveness against the U.S. and others at a level which would enable the farmer to make a rewarding living growing grain. But one should remember that Cargill is playing the very same game in the U.S. and in other countries. How hard is Cargill, or any other such transnational corporation, apt to compete against itself for the benefit of a host country?

In case there is any doubt about the effects of having Cargill operatives in Agriculture Canada, or their similarity of views under the Conservative regime, remember Deputy Minister of Agriculture Noreau's comments on the consistency of Cargill's views with government policy direction *(see page 82)*. Speaking about Cargill's policy reform proposals for transportation, Noreau added,

> The government recognizes that the payment of the Western Grain Transportation Act subsidy to the railways is an impediment to Western diversification . . . A cost-based rate schedule may lead to higher rates westward through the mountains and lower rates eastward. Most of Cargill's activities are in the eastward direction.[125]

Noreau's comment on Cargill's suggestion that "raw product" needs to be unregulated and competitively priced was that, "The government is aware that processors need adequate supplies of competitively priced inputs." This line became embedded as a basic principle of government policy in its document of November, 1989, entitled *Growing Together*. In that document, and in his talks, the idea of a "second generation" of marketing boards was offered as a way out of the contradiction posed by the government's verbal support for marketing boards and the interests of the corporate sector.

As I pointed out earlier, there is nothing novel or even illuminating about the exchange between Cargill and Agriculture Canada, just as the exchange of personnel is simply the way things are done. But the complete agreement in principle on matters of basic policy does suggest that Canadian agriculture policy may be created in corporate boardrooms long before farmers, or the public, are asked to comment. The *Green Paper* cited above, and Agriculture Minister Mazankowski's *National Agri-Food Policy Conference* staged in Ottawa December, 1989, are good examples of this.

Cargill's interest in changing Canadian transportation policy makes good sense for a corporation trying to maximize its opportunities to maximize its profits. In addition to marketing grains as export commodities or domestic feedstuffs, Cargill has a major interest in marketing grain in the form of meat. As indicated in the chronology in Chapter 7, Cargill has consistently pursued a three-level policy based on maximizing returns available on the basis of low grain prices:

• trading grains internationally;

• adding value to cheap grain by using it as the raw material for livestock feed manufacturing;

• adding further value to the cheap grain by turning it into meat.

By positioning itself at each of these three levels, Cargill is able to shift its emphasis from one level to the other depending on current conditions and prices. It has also been policy for some time to secure its position at each level by pursuing a double-track policy of either buying out or driving out its competition while integrating its operations vertically. This has been evident in Cargill's meat operations around the world.

Cargill's interest in radical changes in Canada's historic grain and freight transportation policies is two-fold. First, it sees its own purposes served by concentrating beef production in the west. Thus it works to make it more attractive to finish cattle in Alberta while building the packinghouse able to take advantage of the beef production moving into Alberta. Second, if grain is to be exported from the Prairies, in the long run it is certainly to Cargill's advantage to have the grain handled within its own system to the maximum extent. Thus Cargill would want export grain to move by rail not to Vancouver, but to Thunder Bay or to Minneapolis/St. Paul where it can put the grain on its own barges and take full control over it, or to Lewiston, Idaho or Pasco, Washington, where it would also get onto the water and under Cargill control.

At the same time it wants transportation of grain for domestic consumption, as either feed or food, to be subsidized in the form of payments directly to the farmer so that the farmer will be able to feed it to cattle without the current penalty of having the transport subsidy being paid to the railway so that only grain for export is subsidized. From the standpoint of diversification, of course, Cargill does have a point, but there is a great deal more than this to sustainable agriculture.

Cargill's scenario could easily go like this: work for policy changes that will encourage the production of feed grains in the west. This will provide the basis for a Cargill-dominated beef industry centred on its High River packing plant. At the same time, encourage grain production for export in Ontario where the Canadian Wheat Board does not have jurisdiction and where farmer control of the trade has been all but eliminated. Do this by encouraging payment of the Crow Benefit directly to producers so that they will continue to produce cheap grain, but rather than this going to export it will go into domestic cattle feed where Cargill can capture the "value added". At the same time, work to eliminate all transport and grain production subsides in the east so that Cargill can supply the entire country with beef at low cost and without competition. Grain for export will then be more available for shipment either north to Thunder Bay, south to Minneapolis and into Cargill's barges for shipment down the Mississippi River, southwest to the Columbia River and the West Coast, or east down the St. Lawrence seaway system. To increase the attractiveness of this last option, Cargill has been a member of the coalition lobbying the governments of Canada and the U.S. to make improvements to the St. Lawrence seaway.[126]

A Note on Waterway Maintenance

Cargill's pleasure at the completion of a new lock and dam in the Mississippi River just below Alton, Illinois, where the Mississippi is joined by the Illinois River, was expressed in the lead article in the January 1990 issue of the *Cargill Bulletin*. Cost of the new lock and dam to the U.S. Government was $960-million. The U.S. Army Corps of Engineers, who are responsible for maintaining the 25,000 miles of navigable inland waterways in the U.S., estimate that tonnage on the section of river served by the new lock and dam has increased 10.5% per year and now averages about 70 million tons annually. The article also pointed out that about two-thirds of U.S. exports are shipped from the U.S. Gulf, an area served by the Mississippi.

For comparison, in the 1970's the St. Lawrence Seaway handled about 66 million tonnes annually, though in 1989 it handled only 42 million tones. It, too, is being improved at a cost of some $6-billion to the governments of Canada and the U.S. who operate it jointly.

Chapter 13

GRAINS POLICY

~~~~~~

   As part of its campaign to "allow competitive sourcing of raw products", several years ago Cargill and others succeeded in getting domestic feed barley removed from Wheat Board jurisdiction. Early in 1989 oats was removed altogether. Now Cargill and right-wing grower groups like Western Barley Growers are campaigning to have export barley removed as well.

   As in other aspects of what it makes its business, Cargill did not sit idle waiting for its positions to be adopted. During 1988 and up to the announcement of the decision to remove oats from CWB jurisdiction in mid-1989, letters went back and forth between the Minister responsible for the Wheat Board, Charlie Mayer, and Cargill vice-president Dick Dawson. [127] Various other grain-trade interests also lobbied the government on the issue, as one might expect. In his letter to May of February 29, 1988, Dawson wrote, "Cargill Ltd. proposes that exporters be allowed to contract oats for export directly with farmers for delivery beginning with the 88/89 crop year." Mayer's response, dated April 13, 1988, concluded, "these export opportunities might well be better exploited if the private grain trading firms were able to export directly." Dawson replied in turn, advising Mayer of what the farmers wanted and how to deal with the "small minority" that "will criticize direct sales of oats": "If your office could arrange the right consultative approach, many of the major farm organizations in western Canada would be supportive. The grain trade, of course, would be very supportive."

One of Dawson's "major farm organizations" that he can count on for support is the Western Canadian Wheat Growers Association. Besides sharing the right-wing free-market ideology of Cargill, there are hints that WCWGA has shared in Cargill's financial resources as well. It is reported that its membership is inflated with farmers whose dues are paid by Cargill, or other private traders; be that as it may, according to its own newsletter, *Pro-Farm*,[128] "Four WCWGA representatives attended the sixteenth Farm Leaders Course offered by the Canadian International Grains Institute in Winnipeg... Thanks for financial sponsorship from CN Rail, Parrish and Heimbecker, Cargill Ltd., and Canada Malt Company, costs to WCWGA were kept at a minimum."

This method of providing support to those who will lobby on your behalf in the name of farmers has the obvious advantage of being politically attractive while also allowing the claim that such organizations are not supported by the trade. It is quite unlikely that the books of the WCWGA will show any contributions from corporations like Cargill. And, as I reported earlier, more than one response from people in the grain trade to my questions about Cargill was: "Cargill? I have to do business with them."

Cargill's penchant for anonymity is, again, characterized by an article appearing in *Farm and Country*[129] under the byline of Patrick Lynch, (see p.70). The article is in support of "Plant Breeders' Rights", as they are called, and in it Lynch says, "As long as we are without breeder's rights, there is little encouragement for King Grain, W.G. Thompson, the University of Guelph or federal research stations to increase efforts to breed better disease-resistant varieties." Lynch does not mention Cargill.

A Bigger Slice of the Export Pie

Several years before Cargill's more direct efforts to transform Canadian agricultural policy, it lobbied the government for specific changes which would benefit Cargill as a grain exporter (then its major, if not only, activity in Canada). In April, 1985, Cargill developed a *Position Paper on Export Financing* in which it argued that "Canada's current export financing program is neither competitive nor fair as it applies to the grain industry. The credit grain sales program . . . provides credit only on exports of wheat, barley and oats grown in the Canadian Wheat Board Designated Area."

What Cargill was after was access to government-supported export financing as well as direct access to Canadian grains.

There should be no discrimination against producers of non-Board crops and against producers outside the Designated Area such as the farmer in Ontario growing corn or soft white winter wheat. Moreover, there should be no discrimination against private sector exporters . . .

To this end,

The Government of Canada should establish a broad, competitive and equitable export financing program for grains, oilseeds and related products . . .

In elaborating its argument, Cargill pointed out that the only federal government program supporting export sales of Canadian grains was the Credit Grain Sales program, and that this program was "monopolized" by the Canadian Wheat Board. In calling for a "new, non-discriminatory export financing program", Cargill also suggested that the Canadian International Development Agency (CIDA) program of food aid "could be utilized to promote increased sales of grains, oilseeds, and related products." (As described earlier, Cargill has had many years of experience as the beneficiary of such programs in the U.S, as under Public Law 480.)

Finally, Cargill wrapped this proposal in the flag, so to speak, by saying that it was "required to maintain the competitive position of Canadian farmers . . ."

According to a private report, Cargill maintained a much more visible presence in Ottawa after the Conservatives were elected in 1984. They were assisted in this by Biolink Management Consultants Ltd. (though in 1989 this firm was not listed in either Ottawa or Toronto). Apparently Cargill's lobbying efforts were not in vain. Its wishes, as expressed in the position paper cited above, were at least partially granted through an increase in export financing available from the Export Development Corporation (EDC), though the issue of competitive rates was not fully resolved, at least at that time.

While waiting and working to achieve its long term goals, Cargill has also developed its own infrastructure, so that should it succeed in destroying the Wheat Board and radically altering transportation policy, it would be there to pick up all the pieces.

Its successful efforts to establish itself in the Ontario grain economy are part of this strategy. (In its 1985 *Position Paper* cited above, Cargill pointed out that "Ontario has emerged as a significant grain producer for the export market.") Ontario grain can be utilized either locally or in the U.S. midwest, or it can be exported, under Cargill's control, by water to the Atlantic and beyond, with virtually no rail transport.

Cargill wants to become a national company. And it is diversifying to reduce its dependence on what Kerry Hawkins (President of Cargill) calls "the over-regulated Western grain business".[130]

In late 1989, independent grain elevator operators in Ontario were agreeing that Cargill was setting both the buying and the selling prices of Ontario grains.

Making Sure There Is Too Much

As Cargill has, for years, done its utmost to shape agricultural policy to suit its own corporate goals, abundant cheap, ungraded grain has long been one of its operating premises and objectives. *Laissez faire* is not its policy in regard to grain supplies.

Cargill is well aware of the fact that U.S. grains, unlike Canadian, are not graded for export. It has experienced numerous legal hassles over the sale of grain that has been "extended" by the addition of gravel, dirt, screenings and even water (see quote from 1987 Prospectus on p. 34). Blending of top quality with inferior grain is common practice in the U.S. trade, since the U.S. standards are for minimums only, while Canadian standards are for uniform quality per grade. Since Canada's specialty is top quality, high protein hard spring bread wheat, rather than the lower protein soft winter wheat, it would be to Cargill's advantage to have access to this wheat for blending with inferior U.S. wheats to raise the standard and the price, or to eliminate the Canadian grading standards and the trading advantage enjoyed by the Canadian Wheat Board because of the world-wide reputation of Canadian grains for quality and reliable standards.

For the same reasons, the private traders and their farmer advocates have long called for the Wheat Board to recognize more High Yielding Varieties of wheat as acceptable. The CWB has essentially stuck to its traditional position in favour of accepting varieties of wheat which are visibly uniform and distinguishable in order to maintain the strict quality of the grain it sells.

Besides the adulteration of grains, another route to maximize profits is the use of optional source sales contracts that do not specify the source of the grain being sold, so that the seller can shop around the world, literally, for the best deal before actually having to deliver any grain. Still another tactic is to encourage production wherever possible in order to keep the level of supply high, thus helping to depress the price, it being very hard for suppliers to raise the price when there is a surplus.

In the fall of 1988 Cargill began lobbying for a change in U.S. agricultural policy on the issue of land set-aside for conservation and market management. Cargill philosophy and consequent policy recommendations are clearly stated in its own publication:

> Within the span of just a couple of seasons, the world grain situation has moved from one of "surpluses" in 1986-7 toward a potential "scarcity" . . . The world must find an additional 55-60 million acres in 1989 to protect the world food balance. The United States holds a reserve of highly competitive resources that the world needs. The United States can choose to return its productive resources to a market that is ready and willing to employ them on an ongoing basis, or it can force the U.S. taxpayer to pay to idle those resources indefinitely. It would be wise policy to eliminate acreage reduction programs quickly rather than stand by and watch this opportunity pass to less efficient competitors.[131]

The tight supply/demand balance indicates no acreage should be idled by the 1990 feed-grains program. . . . The tight feed-grain situation in other countries makes U.S. supplies and program decisions even more important. . . . If ever there was a time to unleash the productivity of U.S. agriculture, this is it. . . . Any stock buildup that might occur would provide a welcome increase in food security rather than create a burdensome surplus.[132]

One of the tricks in this trade is to speak as an expert, without arguing the case, as in stating that there is a "tight demand/supply balance". This may or may not be so and in 1989 there were highly divergent views on this issue. It should also be noted that Cargill is deliberately confusing feed grains and food grains: certainly there is a need for food grains, but there is not a market since the hungry cannot afford to purchase their food, even if this were really a solution to the problem of hunger. On the other hand, feed grains are purchased to feed livestock, and since purchased meat is affordable only to a global elite, it is a limited market by definition. So Cargill's argument that more feed grains are needed has nothing to do with "food security". It has to do, rather, with a sector of the grains market that to a great extent should not even exist. The fattening of cattle on grain, after all, only became fashionable in the 1950s when Europe no longer needed massive American food aid and the U.S. was stuck with a surplus of grain. It was only then that the feedlot industry developed. With a swing toward sustainable agriculture, cattle fattened on grain could disappear as suddenly as they appeared, though I cannot imagine Cargill looking forward to such a change. In fact, it is clearly working to not only maintain but even expand the livestock feeding industry.

In this regard, it is worth considering the consequences of the continental "rationalization" of the beef industry. In Canada, for example, until the '80s cattle production was pretty well spread out across the country. Calves and feeder cattle might be concentrated in one region or another, year by year, depending on local circumstances in grain supply and price, but without a clear trend in any one direction. Ecologically this made good sense, and it meant that meat production was regionally oriented and quite self-sufficient in feed.

In the '80s this all changed. With the concentration of cattle finishing and slaughter in Alberta, due to removal of feed grade barley from CWB jurisdiction, provincial subsidies, and most recently the demand created by Cargill's High River plant, Ontario was driven into an increasingly unbalanced concentration on corn and soybean production. From mid-1988 to the end of 1989, slaughter capacity in Ontario dropped from 25,000 head per week to 15,000, and even this is over-capacity.[133] Of the diminishing number of cattle that are slaughtered in Ontario, only 75% or less are raised in the province. This is bad for both the land and the economy in the long run. If the trend continues, the Maritime provinces will be left without a significant livestock industry as well.

It is not only livestock production which is undergoing radical change. Until May, 1989, Cargill was the largest egg producer in the U.S. Then it sold Sunny Foods, its egg production subsidiary that controlled egg production from more than 12-million hens, to Cal-Maine Foods of Jackson, Mississippi. This made Cal-Maine the biggest egg producer in the U.S., with control of some 18-million hens. This "represents a continuing restructuring of egg production into fewer but larger operations:"

> Cargill said that it's selling its shell egg operations because shell eggs no longer fit its long-term strategy . . . James Bassett, president of Cargill's Worldwide Poultry Operations, explained that the company has been repositioning its poultry operations away from commodity products to further-processed, value-added products.[134]

U.S. FUTURES OPTIONS

[—not traded; s—no option offered

Chicago Mercantile Exchange

Chicago Board of Trade

U.S. FUTURES

Chicago Mercantile Exchange

Chicago

Chapter 14

PUBLIC POLICY

Government Meddling at Root of Ag Crisis: Cargill vice-president Dick Dawson said[135] that government policy has led to a "destructive monoculture based on wheat" in Western Canada, delays in plant breeders' rights, and heavy reliance on corn in Ontario. He described free trade with the U.S. as "nothing more than a stepping stone" toward the objective of ridding agriculture of politics and subsidies . . . Dawson rejected the idea that overproduction was at the heart of disrupted trading patterns and weak prices. The problem, he said, lies in food distribution.[136]

Canada must modernize its inefficient western grain handling system and respond to world pressure to change its farming style says Dick Dawson of Cargill. . . . The time for change has come.[137]

In what seems to be a typical pattern for Cargill when it has decided to push a particular global or national agricultural policy, a number of senior Cargill executives make speeches to trade associations and farm groups or give interviews.* Cargill also publishes its own *Cargill Bulletin* (available by subscription), and if one knows the context and reads between the lines, it is possible to discern the public policies which Cargill feels would serve its interests – as I have indicated in my use of the *Cargill Bulletin*.

---

* In the early 1960s Cargill set up a Public Policy Committee within the company which formulates positions on key issues and works out guidelines for the company representatives who speak out publicly.[138]

Usually such policies are presented as being in the best interests of the hungry of the world, a particular country, farmers, or virtually anyone other than Cargill itself.

Thus Kerry Hawkins, president of Cargill Ltd., in an interview for the *Financial Post* of Toronto[139], outlined the Cargill philosophy on agricultural policy:

> There is an emerging consensus that the conventional agricultural policy cures are causing the disease . . . the evidence [not cited] of past policy failure and the logic of economics tells us that we in Canada must support a more market-driven agricultural policy, both domestically and internationally.
>
> I believe a "back to the market" strategy should . . . agree on a set of definitions about what constitutes production and export subsidies. . . and then zero out production and export subsidies.
>
> Major agricultural producing countries should concentrate on devising actuarially sound income insurance policies . . . but we must avoid like the plague commodity-specific programs that encourage overproduction or distort land use decisions.
>
> Farmers will continue to leave agriculture as they have since the beginning of the industrial revolution . . .
>
> Fragile and marginally productive rural land should be retired and protected. In Canada this may mean the creation of a land conservation program which would be established by government to help absorb some of the marginal land now in production [not identified] while cushioning the cost of transition for individual farmers.

During the past couple of years Cargill has been pressing, primarily in the U.S.A., for increased grain production. Its argument has been that the global stockpile is insufficient to prevent catastrophe if there should be significant crop failure anywhere in the world. It urges American policymakers to release more land from set-aside programs and urges farmers to grow more, and more varieties, of grains that are not limited by any government programs (such as quotas or set-asides). At the same time, it has been urging the U.S. to make changes in its programs so that farmers can collect subsidies on land that is taken out of wheat production, for example, but still allowed to be used to produce a crop which Cargill wants more of, like canola. In January, 1990, the U.S. announced just such a change.

Brian Oleson, a Canadian Wheat Board executive, commented on this in a speech to the Western Canadian Wheat Growers Association in January, 1988:

> In recent months, the U.S. private trade has lobbied strongly for increased production and lower idled acreage in order to keep downward pressure on prices. This view is understandable since all costs of this strategy are borne by the public through deficiency payments, export subsidies and storage, while the benefits are reaped by those who earn their profits through storage or movement. This is a no-lose strategy for much of the agri-business sector.

In its September 1989 *Bulletin* Cargill argues its case through the words of Peter Kooi, president, commodity marketing:

> The tight supply/demand balance indicates no acreage should be idled by the 1990 feed grains program . . . Global demand for all grains is growing steadily; total consumption is up 14% since 1980 . . . very little U.S. wheat will be available for livestock feed . . . The tight feedgrain situation in other countries makes U.S. supplies and program decisions even more important. These conditions create a significant opportunity for U.S. agriculture . . . If ever there were a time to unleash the productivity of U.S. agriculture, this is it . . . Any stock build-up that might occur would provide a welcome increase in food security rather than create a burdensome surplus.

What one has to remember is that Cargill's basic business is buying, handling and selling grain. The more grain there is, the more there is to buy and sell. And the more there is, the lower the price to the producer can be in an unregulated and uncompetitive market. It is to Cargill's advantage to have a surplus of grain on the world market, and it consistently pushes for policies and programs that will achieve this goal. There is nothing cynical in this interpretation. The hungry of the world are not customers for Cargill's grain. But cattle producers, including itself, are customers if the price is low enough, and it is feed grains that Cargill is talking about.

Decoupling

A concept that has found new favour with Cargill is "efficient resource allocation". In a speech to the Third Grain Market

Conference in Brussels, June 12, 1987, R. S. Johnson, vice-president, public affairs, Cargill (U.S.), stated:

> [The] long-term goal is to have market forces guide resource allocation ... More attention should be given to easing agricultural adjustment through rural development efforts. And, most important of all, farm incomes should be supported directly rather than through price guarantees ... Decoupling is the only option that relieves all of the building pressures for change.

There are expenses involved in the production of raw materials, if only the wages of those producing the raw materials through the application of their labour. Since land is currently a speculative commodity, and since agricultural inputs are already controlled by a handful of transnational corporations, that leaves only labour uncontrolled by the corporate sector and/or state sector.

This situation has created a challenge for free-enterprise industrial agriculture to come up with schemes whereby the public can subsidize farm labour in an organized and stable fashion. In essence, the program of decoupling calls for putting farmers on welfare and cutting any links between commodity prices and their costs of production. Decoupling would mean the end of supply management. It would bring continued overproduction, low commodity prices, and greater market fluctuations.

> "Decoupling" is a new recipe for delivering government support to agriculture. The [Economic] Council [of Canada] is convinced that a package of programs that decouples farm-production decisions from government programs should be explored. We recognize that such a package would require a major change in the attitudes and traditions of the farming community. And it would necessitate difficult political choices in determining who should receive income support and how the program should be administered. Obviously, that type of change could not be introduced overnight. However, the potential gains to be made in efficiency, self-reliance, and stability of income make decoupling a worthy objective for the medium to longer term.[138]

In *A New Direction for Canada* (Nov. 1984), Canada's finance minister, Michael Wilson, spelled out the agenda of the new Conservative administration:

> First, government policies and programs must be changed to ensure that Canada's private sector can become the driving force of economic renewal in an increasingly competitive marketplace . . . In

some cases, this will mean less government regulation and intervention. In other cases, it will require reducing government subsidies
and other expenditures which undermine the efficient allocation of
our scarce resources.[139]

Daniel Amstutz, the designer of the U.S. position calling for
elimination of all "trade distorting" measures, was previously
head of Cargill Corporation's commodity trading division. It was
Cargill that brought together a number of the largest U.S.
agribusiness firms – Central Soya, Dreyfus, Monsanto, Nabisco –
to form the Agricultural Working Group to lobby for decoupling.

Amstutz defines de-coupling as a government-paid farm income support program where payments are "independent of the
current or future value of a farmer's production and marketings,
input use or commodity prices."

The effect of this would be to have the public, through federal welfare payments to farmers, subsidize the production of
commodities in order to provide a greater profit to the corporate
merchants and processors. Once the transition period was over,
the commodity prices would remain at the new low levels, and
those farmers who continued to produce commodities would have
to subsidize their farm labour themselves, as many do now, with
off-farm work.

The assumption behind decoupling is clearly that farmers
will continue to market their products at a price considerably below the real cost of production, with their real income being
earned by off-farm employment (which will be increasingly hard
to obtain), supplemented by agricultural welfare payments.
(What such commodity prices would do to the development of
agriculture in the Third World is beyond imagining, although one
can imagine how the global food merchants might benefit.)

A drawing of the Greek goddess Demeter (Ceres), from a 5th century red-figure vase. Ceres, the goddess of grain, symbolizes motherhood and the harmony between spiritual and material food.

SECTION VII: MAKING CHOICES

Chapter 15
CONCLUSION

Cargill is certainly not the only force pushing us towards a global monoculture, in the fullest sense of the word, and a global concentration of power. Nor is Cargill solely responsible for the initiatives which are pushing the real prices of farm products lower and lower and creating a profound social crisis in rural Canada.

This rural crisis is also not limited to farming; those with experience in the fishery will quickly see the parallels. The deep-water draggers, like the massive combines, require vast monoculture and capital and are only "efficient" on the basis of marginalizing significant costs – such as depletion of fish stocks and destruction of the ocean floor habitat on the one hand and the draining of sloughs and the elimination of fencerows and wildlife habitat on the other hand – that in the long run must be accounted for. National Sea Products and Cargill bear a striking resemblance to each other in terms of their economic and social functions and their global operations.

Furthermore, what is happening in Canada is little different than what is happening in most of the Third World. It is just a matter of where one is starting – or starving.

As we have seen, the policies and practices of the Conservative government have not served the interests of the Canadian farmer, or indeed of the Canadian public as a whole. This analysis of Cargill's agenda and activities indicates that the close relationship in business and ideology of Cargill and the federal government has not been coincidental. In fact, the steady erosion of Canadian social policy in regard to agriculture may have been due more to the work of Cargill, Ltd., than any other single power in the country.

If this is so, then there seems to be little benefit in continuing to operate on the assumption that the government would do the right thing if only we would tell it what to do. The government *does* do what it is told: by its corporate sponsors, by the farm commodity groups that tell it what it wants to hear, and by the professors and agricultural bureaucrats who are assured of their salaries regardless of how many farmers go bankrupt. Cargill, among others, will provide research funds to universities and pay for farmers to attend "educational" seminars while dishing out a steady stream of slick, and often convincing, propaganda extolling the merits of The Market, of competition, of hybrid seeds and integrated corporations.

Cargill and its corporate peers will continue to flatter those farmers who want to think of themselves as shrewd independent businessmen, but farmers are fooling only themselves if they think they, individually, have any control or power in the face of a massive transnational corporation with very deep pockets, even if they win a skirmish or two:

Cargill's U.S. beef feeding business goes by the name Caprock. A farmer in Kansas, heart of Caprock country, told me a story of a local fabricator and supplier of steel. The local Caprock feedlot was a steady customer, but would never pay its bills in less than thirty days. One day the local business got tired of financing Caprock/Cargill and when the boys turned up for supplies he told them it was now COD. They protested and he simply said, Your credit is no good. Come back with cash and you can pick up your materials. They did come back, with cash, and since then Cargill has paid C.O.D.

For farmers to "compete" with Cargill, or any other TNC, they will have to be equally well organized. Historically, that is why farmers formed the pools and demanded the Wheat Board. Commodity groups which argue and lobby on micro-issues, and compete for political support and public benefits with other commodity groups, while also trying to curry favour with corporate interests, are not the answer.

The issues that Cargill and its accomplices are forcing on the rest of us are not technical issues, nor are they issues of personal preference. The issues that Cargill is deciding for us – or that we will choose to decide for ourselves – are matters of basic morality and social policy. Do we want a competitive individualism that destroys the human community upon which all of us finally depend, or do we want to rebuild our agriculture and our rural society – indeed, our whole society – on the basis of the principles of sustainability and justice and equity for all?

Part of our difficulty in coming to terms with forces like those represented by Cargill is the reductionist logic that has dominated our culture for two centuries. The world is made up of more than bits and pieces randomly associated. The story I have told in this book is one illustration of the way in which everything is connected to and interacts with everything else. Cargill certainly understands this in its corporate mind, and its global operations reflect it, even while many of those who implement corporate policy may remain unaware of how what they do from day to day relates to what other Cargill employees are doing around the world.

From the perspective of this global integration, Cargill may be seen as both powerful and flexible. But its economic power and its political influence are based on only one idea – the unlimited, all-powerful corporation, or empire, with its ideology of profit and efficiency, based on the exploitation of natural resources which are viewed only as commodities.

Of course, the only alternatives it seems reasonable to suggest have radical implications. Reliance on small, localized or bioregional systems would mean rethinking the whole grain economy of Canada. It would certainly mean abandoning wheat monoculture; it might mean turning part (or all) of the prairie back into grassland. Livestock would have a role in an integrated farming system, but feedlots would probably disappear altogether, and along with them centralized slaughtering facilities. Incentives to local production for local consumption would repopulate rural communities. In Ontario, with its prime agricultural land and large industrial workforce, it would mean abandoning the corn/soybean monoculture in favour of genetic diversity and mixed food production for the local/regional market. The shift of food system workers from production to processing would begin to reverse, with less distance between production and consumption.

I am not proposing a blueprint for an alternative to the system represented by Cargill. These are simply elements of a vision which will be fleshed out just as this study of Cargill must be: by research and actions taken at a local or regional level.

The prairie pools, the Wheat Board and other socially controlled marketing structures might still be the best structures to build on, but to meet the threat of the TNCs, like Cargill, will require daring and imagination, and a new realism that understands the power of a vision of justice and community.

We have to consider carefully what our choices might really be – or have to be. We know that we cannot simply carry on with what we have been doing the past 30–40 years. It is not just that our present system of agriculture is vulnerable to corporate control and manipulation because of its divisions into commodities, its dependence on purchased inputs and export monoculture. As I pointed out in From Land to Mouth, it is also leading to the inevitable destruction of our land, air, and water – of our very ability to feed ourselves.

It is not rhetoric, but common sense, to seek radical alternatives.

THE ELEVATOR. PORT Mc NICOLL. ONT.. CANADA

Postcard courtesy J.G. Young (Port McNicoll Library)

Afterword

January 1, 1990, Port McNicoll, Ontario:

This small town on Georgian Bay will lose its only industry, a third of its tax base and a historic landmark . . . The Port McNicoll grain elevator, built near the turn of the century by ancestors of many of the people who live in this town of 2000, will be blown up this spring . . . Until the 1960s, the Port McNicoll elevator was the largest grain storage building in the world . . . Cargill Grain Co. of Winnipeg announced last week it will demolish the elevator . . . Two other grain elevators will close this winter in Midland, five kilometres away.[139]

Cargill acquired the Port McNicoll and Midland elevators when it bought Maple Leaf Mills grain division from Hillsdown holdings in early 1899. In October, 1989, Cargill sold an option on the Port McNicoll elevator and its adjacent 35 hectare parcel of land to R.J. Kemp Management Co. Ltd. of Toronto. Kemp said it plans to build a $100-million condominium on the site.[140]

These plans may not materialize because Canadian Pacific owns 700 acres of land that provide the only access to the terminal. Several years ago CP transferred the terminal and site, on a point of land with water on three sides, first to its subsidiary, Marathon Realty, and then to Maple Leaf Mills, another CP division. In addition, bids for demolition of the elevator run from $4- to 8-million. In the meantime, Cargill is contesting its tax bill with the town.

In December, 1989, Cargill notified its employees in Port McNicoll that they would not be needed after Jan. 31, 1990. I was told that the employees were not offered jobs in other Cargill facilities, were given no help in retraining or placement and were given no severance pay.

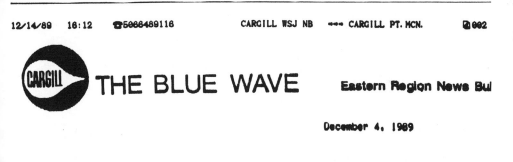

12/14/89   16:12   ☎5066489116   CARGILL WSJ NB   •••• CARGILL PT. MCN.   ☒002

THE BLUE WAVE   Eastern Region News Bul

December 4, 1989

EASTERN REGION ANNOUNCEMENT

The grain transfer terminal at Port McNicoll will cease operations effective January 31st, 1990. No grain shipments are available for the facility this winter and therefore no work is available for employees. Due to reductions in transportation subsidies and other developments in the grain industry, very little prospect of future need for an export oriented transfer terminal in the Georgian Bay is foreseen.

Courtesy Port McNicoll Library

Author's Footnote:

This is not the end, but the beginning of the process which will tell the full, global story of Cargill. You are invited to share your own stories and research; I can be reached through NC Press.

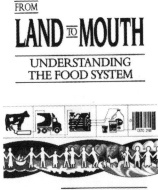

Also by Brewster Kneen:

FROM LAND TO MOUTH:
Understanding the Food System
176 pages, paperback, $14.95 – available from:

NC Press
(416) 593-6284

ENDNOTES

Note: Dates are entered: day/month/year

Introduction

(1) Cargill Prospectus, 1987
(2) *Forbes*, 11/12/89
(3) *Ontario Farmer*, 4/10/89
(4) company brochure, Sept. 1989
(5) Auer, 1989, p.60
(6) Furtan et al, 1989, p.75
(7) *Handling the Risks*, 1988

Chapter 2

(8) CWB publication, no date
(9) Fairbairn, 1984, p.209
(10) Fairbairn, 1984, p.208
(11) *Globe & Mail* 19/1/89, 25/1/89
(12) Executive Summary, *Sask. Wheat Pool Public Policy for Agriculture*, 1989
(13) National Grains Bureau information and *Western Producer*, 14/4/88
(14) Fulton, p.28
(15) Skogstad, 1987, p.30
(16) Fairbairn, 1984, p. 214-5
(17) Mitchell, 1975, p.18
(18) *Manitoba Co-operator*, 11/1/90
(19) *Western Producer*: 15/1/87, 14/1/88
(20) NGB information
(21) Western Canadian Wheat Growers Association – "Lobbying, Research, Education: *It Pays To Belong*", Regina, Sask., 1986/7 (no date)
(22) *Pro-Farm*, June 1989, p.19
(23) *Assessment of the Attitudes of the Prairie Farming Community*, April 1989, p.51
(24) ibid., p. 11
(25) Prince Albert Caucus, 5/7/84, *P.C. Agenda for Government*
(26) *Assessment of the Attitudes*, p.14
(27) ibid., p.17
(28) loc. cit.

Chapter 3

(29) phone interview, R. Bethune, 3/1/90 & U.C.O. *1989 Annual Report*
(30) *Milling & Baking News*, 21/11/89
(31) Gilmore, 1982, p.60

Chapter 4

(32) *Forbes*, 18/9/78

(33) 26/10/87
(34) 23/10/89
(35) "Presentation to Finance Canada", 24/2/89
(36) Prospectus, 1987
(37) Library of Parliament
(38) *Farm and Country*, 10/10/89 & *Ontario Farmer*, 4/10/89
(39) interview with Cargill chairman Whitney MacMillan in the *New York Times*, 30/3/86
(40) *Feedstuffs*, 24/4/89
(41) 11/4/89
(42) *Cargill Bulletin*, Sept. 1989
(43) *Forbes*, 18/9/78
(44) company brochure, Ontario, fall, 1989
(45) Whitney MacMillan, Chairman, Cargill Inc., quoted in the *St. Paul Pioneer Press Dispatch*, 9/5/88

Chapter 5

(46) Wessel, 1983, pp.152-3. See also pp. 91-109
(47) *Financial Times*, in *Globe & Mail*, 3/12/86
(48) *Milling & Baking News*, 22/8/89
(49) *Milling & Baking News*, 14/11/89
(50) *Globe & Mail 24/6/88*
(51) *Western Producer 30/6/88*
(52) 29/8/89
(53) *Globe & Mail 13/1/87*
(54) *Western Producer*, 17/8/89
(55) *Milling & Baking News* 28/11/89

Chapter 6

(56) Merchants of Grain, 1979
(57) Burbach & Flynn, p. 240
(58) *Forbes*, 18/9/78
(59) *Un plan Marshall contre l'usure financière*, Dec. 1987
(60) Gilmore, p.138
(61) *Cargill Bulletin*, Oct. 1988
(62) Family Farm Organizing Resource Centre, St.Paul, no date
(63) *Forbes*, 17/11/86
(64) *Oils and Fats International*, Issue Two, 1988
(65) *Han-kyoreh Shinmun*, 24/8/89, translation
(66) *Korea Times*, 28/9/89
(67) *Milling & Baking News*, 12/12/89

Chapter 7

(68) Newman, 1982, pp.224 ff.
(69) Yaworski, 1976
(70) *Business Week*, 16/4/79

(71) *Globe & Mail 12/11/81*
(72) *Globe & Mail, 8/2/82*
(73) *Western Producer*, 17/6/82
(74) Dick Dawson, quoted in *Western Producer*, 28/2/86
(75) *Western Producer*, 28/8/86
(76) *Globe & Mail*, 21/11/89

Chapter 8

(77) May, 1989
(78) Annual Report, 1988
(79) *Globe & Mail* 8/2/90
(80) *Globe & Mail* 3/11/89
(81) *Feedstuffs*, 21/8/89
(82) *Ontario Farmer*, 16/11/88
(83) *Financial Post*, 27-29/1/90
(84) *Western Producer*, 16/11/89
(85) *Western Producer*, 5/2/90
(86) *Korea Times*, 12/10/89
(87) *Canadian Grocer*, Aug. 1989
(88) *Forbes*, 19/2/90
(89) *Farm and Country*, 21/11/89
(90) Cargill promotion, no date
(91) *Western Producer* 14/9/89, *Farm Journal* Nov. 1989

Chapter 9

(92) Jack McEowan of Michigan State University, speaking to a meeting of the Ontario Grain and Feed Dealers Association – *Ontario Farmer*, 21/6/89
(93) according to Brian Doidge of Ridgetown College of Agricultural Technology
(94) Interview, 3/6/88
(95) *Farm and Country*, 13/2/90
(96) *Milling and Baking News*, 28/11/89
(97) *The Economist*, 29/7/89
(98) *Manitoba Co-operator* 16/11/89
(99) *Cargill Bulletin*, March 1989
(100) *Western Producer*, 7/2/85
(101) private file, Pat Roy Mooney
(102) *Farm and Country*, 10/5/88
(103) *Financial Post*, 12/9/88
(104) phone interview, 2/12/89
(105) Memorandum of Information, 28/2/89
(106) Burbach & Flynn, page 250
(107) *Business Week*, 18/9/89
(108) *Western Producer*, 30/11/89
(109) Yaworski, 1976

(110) *Toronto Star*, 9/12/89

Chapter 11

(111) *Cargill Bulletin*, Nov. 1988
(112) Yaworski, 1976
(113) *Western Producer*, 25/11/82
(114) Gilmore, p.119
(115) Gilmore, p.123
(116) *Milling & Baking News*, 6/6/89

Chapter 12

(117) Yaworski, 1976
(118) Brian Doidge, Ridgetown College of Agricultural Technology, *Ontario Farmer*, 10/1/90
(119) *Western Producer*, 27/7/89
(120) *Western Producer*, 21/9/89
(121) Budget, 13/1/89
(122) *Western Producer*, 16/9/76
(123) "commercial strawberry grower" Dennis Rice in *Grainnews*, January 1990, p.32
(124) 24/2/89
(125) Memorandum of Information, 28/2/89
(126) *Western Producer*, 1/6/89

Chapter 13

(127) *Saskatoon Star-Phoenix*, 20/7/89
(128) April, 1989
(129) 21/11/89
(130) *Financial Post*, 15/8/88
(131) *Cargill Bulletin*, Nov. 1988
(132) *Cargill Bulletin*, Sept. 1989
(133) *PDR Notes*, Ontario Ministry of Agriculture and Food, 8/12/89
(134) *Feedstuffs*, 19/6/89

Chapter 14

(135) speech in Chatham in May, 1987
(136) *Ontario Farmer*, 17/6/87
(137) *Western Producer*, 17/11/88
(138) Burbach & Flynn, page 248
(139) 26/1/87
(140) "A Report on the Prairie Grain Economy", Economic Council of Canada, 1988, p. 77
(141) "A New Direction for Canada", p. 83

Chapter 15

(142) *Toronto Star*, 1/1/90

BIBLIOGRAPHY

Agriculture Canada, Deputy Minister: Memorandum of Information – Analysis of Cargill Brief on Agriculture Policy, Feb. 28, 1989 (3 pages)

Ahlberg, Brian: "Cargill: The Invisible Giant", *Multinational Monitor*, July/Aug. 1988 (4 pages)

Auer, Ludwig: Canadian Prairie Farming, 1960-2000, An Economic Analysis, Economic Council of Canada, 1989

Burbach, Roger & Flynn, Patricia, Agribusiness in the Americas, Monthly Review Press and North American Congress on Latin America, 1980

Canadian Grain Commission, Winnipeg, Annual Report, 1986

Canadian Grains Industry Statistical Handbook 89, Canada Grains Council, Winnipeg, 1989

Canadian Wheat Board: The Canadian Wheat Board, booklet, no date

Cargill, Incorporated: Prospectus, 1987

Cargill Ltd.: Presentation to Finance Canada, Feb. 24, 1989, 18 pages

Cargill Ltd.: corporate publicity 33 pages, no date (c.1985)

Cargill Ltd.: 60th Anniversary promotion broadsheet, 16 pages, 1988

Cargill World of Juices: trade promotion, no date (c.1988)

Carter, C., McCalla, A.F., Schmitz, A.: Canada and International Grain Markets: Trends, Policies, and Prospects, Economic Council of Canada, 1989

Commission Agricole de l'Institut Schiller: *Un plan Marshall contre l'usure financière*, Paris, 1987

Decima Research: "Assessment of the Attitudes of the Prairie Farming Community", A study for Prairie Pools, Inc., 1989

Dun and Bradstreet Consolidated Report: Cargill Inc., May 19, 1986 (six pages)

Economic Council of Canada: Handling the Risks – a Report on the Prairie Grain Economy, 1988

Elections Canada Bureau: Contributions of Agribusinesses (no date, 6 pages)

Fairbairn, G.: From Prairie Roots – The Remarkable Story of Saskatchewan Wheat Pool, Western Producer Prairie Books, 1984

Family Farm Organizing Resource Center, St. Paul, MN, c.1986, 12 pages, (no title or date)

Fulton, M., Rosaasen, K., Schmitz, A.: <u>Canadian Agricultural Policy and Prairie Agriculture</u>, a study prepared for the Economic Council of Canada, 1989

Furtan, W.H., Bayri, T.Y.,Gray, R., Storey, G.G.: <u>Grain Market Outlook</u>, a study prepared for the Economic Council of Canada, 1989

Gilmore, Richard: <u>A Poor Harvest</u>, Longman, 1982

Johnson, Robbin S. (v.p., public affairs, Cargill Inc.) speech to the Third Grain market Conference, Brussels, June 1987

Juma, Calestous: <u>The Gene Hunters – Biotechnology and the Scramble for Seeds</u>, Princeton University Press, 1989

KPMG Peat Marwick: Non-Consolidated Financial Statements of Cargill Ltd., Year Ended May 31, 1989

Krebs, A.V., <u>Cargill: the Peoples' Report</u>, 1988 (90 pages, no location)

Library of Parliament, computer printout financial summary, Cargill Ltd., 15/06/89

McDonald, Dale: "No Mercy from the Multinationals", *Top Producer*, November, 1987 (4 Pages)

Mitchell, Don: <u>The Politics of Food</u>, Lorimer, 1975

Morgan, Dan, <u>Merchants of Grain</u>, Viking Press, 1979; Penguin, 1980

National Grains Bureau, publicity, 1990

Newman: <u>The Establishment Man</u>, McClelland and Stewart, 1982

New Republic: "The Grain Drain - Cargill's Private Empire", Dec. 18, 1976

Oleson, Brian T., "World Grain Trade: An Economic Perspective Of The Current Price War", speech to American Agricultural Economics Association and the Canadian Agricultural Economics Association, August 1987

Pearce, Wm. R. (senior v.p., Cargill Inc) spech to the European-American Journalists Conference, Copenhagen, July 1987

Port of Stockton (Calif.): promotional booklet, 1989, 74 pages

<u>Profile on Cargill Incorporated</u>, Stichting Onderzoek Multinationale Ondernemingen (SOMO), private report, Amsterdam, 1988

Pugh, Terry: "Down the Corporate Road – Prairie wheat pools and free trade", *Briarpatch*, January 1989

Saskatchewan Wheat Pool: "Public Policy for Agriculture – Major Issues for 1990"

Skogstad, Grace: <u>The Politics of Agricultural Policy-making in Canada</u>, Univ. of Toronto Press, 1987

Slinkard and Fowlers, eds.: <u>Wheat Production in Canada – A Review</u>, Division of Extension and Community Relations, U. of Saskatchewan, 1986 [note corporate sponsors, with Cargill at top of list]

Veeman and Veeman: <u>The Future of Grain</u> – Canadian Institute for Economic Policy & Lorimer, 1984

Wessel, James: <u>Trading the Future – Farm Exports and the Concentration of Economic Power</u>, Institute for Food and Development Policy, 1983

Yaworski, Brian: <u>A Corporate Analysis of Cargill Incorporated</u>, May 1976 (33 pages, no location)

Western Canadian Wheat Growers Association – "Lobbying, Research, Education: It Pays To Belong", Regina, Sask., 1986/7 (no date)

Periodicals:

Business Week, April 16, 1979

Cargill Bulletin, monthly, (available by subscription), P.O. Box 9300, Minneapolis, MN 55440, U.S.A.

Cargill News, (no frequency stated, an internal publication of Cargill) PO. Box 9300, Minneapolis, MN 55440, U.S.A.

International Labour Reports, "Profit Fodder", July-Aug. 1987 (five pages)

Financial Post, Toronto

Forbes, weekly

Globe and Mail, Toronto, daily

Grainews, United Grain Growers, Winnipeg, monthly

Manitoba Co-Operator, Winnipeg, weekly

Milling and Baking News, Marriam Kansas, U.S.A., weekly (trade journal)

Ontario Farmer, London, Ont., weekly

Pro-Farm, Western Canadian Wheat Growers Association, Regina, bi-monthly

Toronto Star, daily

Western Producer, Saskatoon, Sask., weekly

INDEX

Agricultural Working Group 115

Agriculture Canada 19, 20, 76, 81, 82, 99, 100

Agro-Tex Commodities Inc. 49

Alberta 2, 5, 13, 15, 16, 54, 58, 63-66, 71, 95, 96, 100, 109

Alberta Wheat Pool 15, 16

Amstutz 83, 115

Andre/Garnac 27

Archer Daniels Midland (ADM) 28, 72-75, 93

Argentina 4, 43, 54, 76, 83

Arkona Feed Mills Ltd. 61

Asgrow 52, 70

At-and-East 94

Australia 4

Ayr Feed and Supply 54

Baie Comeau 51-53

Belle Plaine 57, 58, 60

blending 54, 106, 107

Brazil 27, 48, 88

British Columbia 2, 13, 16, 67

Bunge and Born 27, 75, 83, 84

Burford Fertilizer 57

Burns Foods 67

Business Council on National Issues 8

Cal-Maine Foods 109

Canada Grains Council 16

Canada Packers 64, 67, 73

Canadian 88 Energy Corp. 58

Canadian Alliance for Trade and Job Opportunities 85

Canadian Cattlemen's Association 20, 21

Canadian Dressed Meats 67

Canadian Grain Commission 16

Canadian International Trade Tribunal 21

Canadian National railway 96

Canadian Wheat Board (CWB) 2, 4, 5, 8, 9, 13-16, 18, 19, 21, 24, 25, 44, 52, 53, 70, 74, 82, 89, 90, 93-95, 97, 101, 103, 105, 107, 109, 113

Canagrain 28

canola 72, 75-77, 90, 99, 112

Canola Inc. 75

Caprock 48, 118

Cargill Foods 65, 66, 81

Cargill Hybrid Seeds 52

Cargill Pork Systems 67

Cargill Port 58, 59, 98

Carla Hills 49

Carter administration 49

Chicago Board of Trade (CBOT) 25, 39, 73, 74

Child 67

China 44, 65

ConAgra 28, 64

Continental Grain 16, 28, 43, 44

Crows Nest Pass freight rate 91, 94

CVOP 73

Cyanamid 16, 33, 56, 57, 69, 79

Dawson, Dick 53, 63, 84, 86, 96, 99, 103, 104, 111

de Kemp, Phil 81, 82

Decima Research 23, 24

decoupling 113-115

Dixon, California 80

Dreyfus 10, 27, 35, 44, 115

Ducks Unlimited 64

Economic Council of Canada 5, 10, 20, 114

eggs 21, 52, 109

Elders 28, 29

European Community (EC) 4, 5, 43, 44, 68

Excel 48, 64, 66, 68

Executive Exchange Program 81, 82

Export Development Corporation 106

Export Enhancement Program (E.E.P.) 43-45

External Affairs 19, 82

Fair, Milt 93

Feed Freight Assistance 94

Feruzzi 72-75

Food for Peace 41
Food Security Act 43
Foreign Agricultural Service 43
Foreign Investment Review Agency 8
From Land To Mouth 11, 120

Gairdinier 61
GATT 83
Gillies, Ian 70
Gilmore, David 81
Gilmore, Richard 48, 90, 91
Grain Marketing Bureau 19, 82
Grains 2000 20
Grains and Oilseeds 17-20, 22, 23, 81, 94, 95
Grains Group 21
Growing Together 99

Hanna Mining 51, 52
Hawkins, Kerry 2, 37, 74, 86, 106, 112
hedging 8, 34, 39, 40, 70, 74
High Fructose Corn Syrup (HFCS) 48, 71
High River, Alberta 63-67, 81, 101, 109
Hillsdown Holdings 54, 55

IBP 64
intellectual property rights 33
Investment Canada 8
invisible hand 11
Isman, Barbara 22, 58, 65, 69, 70, 71, 79, 82

Johnson, Robbin 87, 114
Kemp Management 121
Kerr Gifford 51
Kola Feeds 54

Lakeside Packers 64
Lang, Otto 17, 21 , 52, 95
Lynch, Pat 70, 104

MacMillan 32, 37, 40, 41
Manitoba 2, 5, 13, 21, 54, 67
Manitoba Co-operator 21
Manitoba Pool Elevators 15, 16
Maple Leaf Mills 28, 54, 55, 69, 75, 80, 121
Marshall Plan 41

Mayer, Charlie 16, 18, 20, 23, 81, 82, 103
MBPXL 48
McEwan, Harvey 23
Menem (Argentina) 83, 84
Merieux Group 54
Minneapolis 1, 35, 37, 58, 59, 87, 101
Minnesota 1, 37, 87
Minnetonka 1
Mississippi River 58, 88, 101, 102
Mitsui/Cook 27
Moncton 2, 65
Mosbacher 49
Mount Lehman 67
Mulroney, Brian 52
Murray, Roger 52, 53, 85

National Association of Wheat Growers 43
National Grain 25, 52, 83, 84, 94
National Grains Bureau 19, 20, 22
National Sea Products 117
National Starch of Canada 76
New Brunswick 2, 54
Nipigon Transport 51
Nippon Meat Packers 50
Noreau, Jean Jacques 82, 99
Nutrena 52

Oleson, Brian 113
Ontario 2, 3, 9, 12, 16, 20, 22, 25, 28, 33, 37, 40, 52-54, 57, 58, 61, 63, 66, 67, 69-71, 73, 75, 76, 79, 80, 93, 101, 105, 106, 109, 111, 120, 121
Ontario Corn Producers' Association 20
Ontario Wheat Marketing Board 9, 25, 28, 70
orange juice 88

P.A.G. Seeds 52
Palliser Triangle Wheat Growers' Association 20, 21
Panama 34, 35
Panco Poultry 53
Parrish & Heimbecker 16
Pasco, Washington 89, 101
Paterson, N.M. 16
Peace River 13

Philippines 49
Pioneer Grain 16, 21, 94
Potash Corp. of Saskatchewan 60
Prairie Pools Inc. 23
Prince Rupert 16, 36
producer cars 90, 91
Public Law 480 41, 42, 105
Puerto Rico 48

Quebec 2, 22, 51, 57, 58

Rapanelli 83
Redpath 71
Richardson, James & Sons 16, 85, 86, 94
Rogers Terminal and Shipping Co. 88
Royal Bank 16

Saferco Products 57, 60
Saskatchewan 2, 5, 13, 15, 16, 18, 22, 23, 29, 54, 58-61, 93
Saskatchewan Wheat Pool 15, 16, 18, 19, 22, 29, 58, 93
SaskPower 58, 59
Shaver Poultry 50, 52, 54
Smith 11
social Darwinism 11, 12
South Korea 49
Southern Feeds 54
St. Lawrence seaway 51, 101, 102
St. Lawrence Starch 71
Staley 71
Stockton, California 63, 88
Sunny Foods 109
sustainable oligopoly 27, 28

Targeted Export Assistance Program 43
Tate and Lyle 71
Thailand 47, 50
Thunder Bay 3, 16, 51-53, 69, 98, 101
Tradax 34, 35, 47

U.S. Department of Agriculture 43, 44
U.S. Feed Grains Council 43
U.S. Wheat Associates 43
UN Relief and Rehabilitation Agency 41

Unilever 76
unit train 90
United Cooperatives of Ontario (UCO) 28, 73
United Grain Growers (UGG) 16, 17, 28, 29, 96
Upjohn 52

Vancouver 2, 16, 51, 58, 101
variable rates 90, 91
Victory Soya Mills 72

Western Barley Growers 90, 103
Western Canadian Wheat Growers Association 16, 18, 20, 22, 23, 82, 90, 104, 113
Western Grain Transportation Act 94, 97, 99
Wheat Board 2, 4, 5, 8, 9, 13-19, 21, 23-25, 44, 52, 53, 70, 74, 82, 89, 93, 94, 101, 103, 105-107, 113, 119, 120
Will Cargill 41
Wilson 83, 84, 114
Winnipeg 2, 16, 20, 21, 35, 51, 82, 104, 121
Winnipeg Grain Exchange 16

XCan Grain Ltd. 17
XL 65

Yeutter, Clayton 44